"The authors' extensive international experience will facilitate effective collaboration between educators, professionals and parents to create effective programs for students with disabilities."

Temple Grandin, *author of* Visual Thinking: The Hidden Gifts of People Who Think in Pictures, Patterns, and Abstractions

"I expected this book to speak to my intellect and to my practice. The best professional texts do that. Boll and Ly's *Navigating Special Education Relationships* went beyond. It spoke to my heart. The best colleagues do that."

Cornelius Minor, *Brooklyn-based educator and author*

"*Navigating Relationships in Special Education* reminds us that when educators work together and believe in the goodness of people, we can truly make a difference in this world."

Tim Villegas, *Director of Communications, Maryland Coalition for Inclusive Education (MCIE) Founder of Think Inclusive*

"It is difficult to think of a more comprehensive and helpful book on the complex dimensions of special education. The power of this book is two-fold. First, it offers rich, up-to-date information. Even more importantly, the book was created by caring individuals who, themselves, have experienced firsthand the challenges of teaching children with exceptionalities as well as having lived through the experience of being parents of children with special needs. This book is indeed a gift to all educators and parents who seek the understanding required to support children with exceptionalities today."

Edward E. Greene, *Ph.D. Executive Director EARCOS (East Asia Regional Council of Schools)*

"The authors provide an honest and important discussion with regards to many factors which make it difficult for children with Autism Spectrum and learning differences to be diagnosed and educated within our public and private schools. They also offer important tips to parents to help them anticipate some of the hurdles they may encounter as well as tips for how best to navigate through them."

Michelle Garcia Winner, *MA-CCC Founder of the Social Thinking Methodology Speech Language Pathologist*

"Drawing upon their vast expertise in international education, these authors skillfully navigate the intricate terrain of inclusive education, blending personal experiences with in-depth analysis and expertise. Their profound understanding of global educational dynamics enriches the discourse, making the chapters an essential read for anyone within the field of international education."

Dana Specker Watts, *Ph.D. Director of Learning,*
Research and Outreach
International School Services (ISS)

Navigating Special Education Relationships

Told through a series of real-life stories and hard-learned lessons, Amanda Ly and Lori Boll share the challenges in special education relationships experienced through the lens of a special educator, a parent of a son with profound disabilities, and a child psychologist.

Ideally, teachers, therapists, and parents working with students with special needs should form a cohesive team. However, these three parties often function as separate entities with different goals and objectives. Over the past 25 years, the authors have observed a consistent pattern of miscommunication and overlooking the importance of the mental and physical well-being of each team member, which contributed to poor collaboration. This book takes readers on a journey through the process of discovering whether you have, or are working with, a student with special needs; navigating how to best work with the student and other members of the team; and lastly, discussing ways to empower the reader and all members of the team. The authors posit that if we understand one another's perspectives, learn how to communicate more effectively, and focus on self-care, we will increase Collective Efficacy and become the collaborative team our students need us to be.

As the first book to connect the concept of Collective Efficacy to special education, this is a must-read for teachers, therapists, and parents aiming to grasp the complexities of relationships in special education teams and better understand how mental health influences the effectiveness of each individual's role.

Amanda Ly holds a PhD in School Psychology and Board Certification in Behavior Analysis-Doctoral (BCBA-D) and has worked in private and group practices throughout the United States, China, and Singapore. She is a parent of a typically developing daughter and a child psychologist, bringing over 22 years of rich experience working with young people with various disabilities.

Lori Boll holds two master's degrees in Reading and Special Education and has taught in the United States, Saipan, Saudi Arabia, Indonesia, China, and Thailand. She is the mother of a daughter and an adult son with profound autism, shaping her core beliefs around supporting all learners and their families. Lori has presented at multiple international educational conferences. She is currently the Executive Director of the Special Education Network and Inclusion Association (SENIA).

Navigating Special Education Relationships

Building Collective Efficacy for a Collaborative Team

Amanda Ly, Ph.D., BCBA-D and
Lori Boll, M.Ed.

LONDON AND NEW YORK

Designed cover image: Getty Images

First published 2024
by Routledge
4 Park Square, Milton Park, Abingdon, Oxon OX14 4RN

and by Routledge
605 Third Avenue, New York, NY 10158

Routledge is an imprint of the Taylor & Francis Group, an informa business

© 2024 Amanda Ly and Lori Boll

The right of Amanda Ly and Lori Boll to be identified as authors of this work has been asserted in accordance with sections 77 and 78 of the Copyright, Designs and Patents Act 1988.

All rights reserved. No part of this book may be reprinted or reproduced or utilised in any form or by any electronic, mechanical, or other means, now known or hereafter invented, including photocopying and recording, or in any information storage or retrieval system, without permission in writing from the publishers.

Trademark notice: Product or corporate names may be trademarks or registered trademarks, and are used only for identification and explanation without intent to infringe.

British Library Cataloguing-in-Publication Data
A catalogue record for this book is available from the British Library

ISBN: 978-1-032-63433-3 (hbk)
ISBN: 978-1-032-63428-9 (pbk)
ISBN: 978-1-032-63435-7 (ebk)

DOI: 10.4324/9781032634357

Typeset in Times New Roman
by SPi Technologies India Pvt Ltd (Straive)

This book is dedicated to our greatest teachers, our children – Madi Boll, Braden Boll, and Hedy Ly

Contents

List of Illustrations   xi
Author Biographies   xii
Foreword   xiv
Acknowledgments   xvii

Introduction to *Navigating Special Education Relationships*   1

PART I
Discovering   7

1. Collective Efficacy   9
2. Discovering a Disability: Sniffing Socks and an Autism Diagnosis   15
3. Discovering the Diagnosis Dilemma: To Label or Not   20
4. Discovering Complications With the Diagnosis Process: The Gatekeeper Problem   27
5. Discovering Prevalence Rates and Screening Tools   30
6. Discovering the Diagnostic Assessment Process   34
7. Discovering the Diagnostic Process in School Settings: Multi-Tiered System of Supports (MTSS)   46
8. Discovering Concerns and Fears: Supporting General Education Teachers   50
9. Discovering the Realities of a Diagnosis: It's Hard   59

PART II
Navigating 69

10 Navigating Through the Educational Jargon: Enough With the Acronyms Already 71

11 Navigating Concerns Relating to Educational Setting: School Placement and Goodness of Fit 75

12 Navigating School Transitions 81

13 Navigating Mistrust: Presume Competence 88

14 Navigating Professional Relationships: I've Been Teaching Longer Than You've Been Alive, Honey 100

15 Navigating Through Misguided Notions: Golden Ticket 105

16 Navigating Different Schools of Thought: Old School Versus New School 109

17 Navigating Bias: There's No Such Thing as a Lazy Kid 116

18 Navigating Relationships With the Most Important Member of Our Team: Fake It 'Til You Make It 120

19 Navigating Miscommunication: Mind the Gap 125

20 Navigating Team Success: Yes. We Can 131

PART III
Empowering 137

21 Empowering You to Have a Difficult Conversation: Turn In 139

22 Empowering Confidence: Imposter Syndrome 147

23 Empowering Your Mental and Physical Health: Self-Care 160

References *175*
Index *179*

Illustrations

Figures

6.1	Flow Chart Dr. Ly Comprehensive Diagnostic Assessment	36
6.2	Cast a Wide Net to Rule In or Out	36
6.3	Guideline for Best Practice in Assessment	37
6.4	Sources of Informants	37
6.5	Diagnosis Confirmed	38
6.6	Diagnosis Contradicted	38
6.7	Diagnosis Inconclusive	39
6.8	Standard Normal Curve	41
6.9	Cognitive Abilities Within the Normal Range	41
6.10	Cognitive Abilities Within the Borderline Clinically Significant Range	42
6.11	Cognitive Abilities Significantly Below the Mean and of Clinical Concern	42
6.12	Cognitive Abilities Significantly Above the Mean aka Giftedness	43
7.1	Multi-Tiered System of Supports (MTSS)	47
8.1	IEP at a Glance	54
8.2	Example of Class-Wide Student Accommodations at a Glance	55
8.3	Universal Design for Learning UDL	57
13.1	Daily Communication Log Example	98
21.1	ATTUNE	140
23.1	Seven Pillars of Self-Care	166
23.2	Different Styles of Yoga	172

Tables

5.1	Prevalence Rates of Select Special Needs Categories	31
12.1	School and Family Point of View on School Placement	85
13.1	Requirements for Various Special Education Professionals	92
13.2	Examples for Data Gathering	93

Author Biographies

Amanda Ly is a parent of a typically developing daughter and a seasoned child psychologist, bringing over 22 years of rich experience working with young people with various disabilities. Beginning her career in the United States, Amanda's expertise has taken her to China, back across the United States, and then abroad to Singapore. She has worked in an array of settings including residential facilities, clinics, and home environments, focusing her career on autism and development disorders. Holding a PhD and Board Certification in Behavior Analysis, Amanda's passion lies in identifying the unique challenges faced by children with disabilities and their families. Her main passion is to assist families in understanding their personal circumstances, making the journey as informed and ease filled as possible. Amanda's commitment to helping families navigate through the complex world of diagnosis and treatment has positioned her as a trusted expert in her field. Her strength in connecting with families and her dedication to providing them with the tools and information they need are the cornerstones of her practice.

Lori Boll is an internationally recognized speaker and leader in special education, boasting over 25 years of experience. Holding two graduate degrees in reading education and special education, her extensive teaching career spans the globe including Saipan, Saudi Arabia, Indonesia, China, Thailand, and the United States.

Lori is the mother of two children, Madi and Braden. Her personal connection to individuals with disabilities deepened profoundly in 2003 when Braden was diagnosed with autism spectrum disorder (ASD) and an intellectual developmental delay (IDD). This catalyzed a shift in Lori's career, transforming her from an elementary teacher to a fervent advocate for all children and inclusive education. She served as principal of a school for special needs in Shanghai, China and later cofounded the city's first inclusive school. In 2017, she created the inaugural higher support needs program at the International School Bangkok, extending her influence to schools globally.

Currently serving as Executive Director of SENIA International, Lori continues to champion the rights and resources for students with disabilities. SENIA advocates for neurodiverse and disabled individuals, empowers educators, professionals, and family members, and fosters connections in the global community. Lori also contributes as an associate faculty member for the counselling department at Oregon State University, Cascades.

Lori has walked the path that many families are just beginning and feels ready to advocate for not just the children with whom she's worked for over 25 years but their families, therapists, and teachers as well.

Foreword

A Call to Inclusion: From "I" to "We Winned" in Education

Katie Novak

I consider myself incredibly blessed to have a vibrant, brilliant daughter with complex ADHD. From the moment she could walk and talk, she was a firecracker. On two unforgettable occasions, we triggered a "Code Adam," a store lockdown. After an intense search, we found our little Houdini hiding in a clothing display, grinning from ear to ear, proudly declaring, "I winned!" She clearly expected a different reception for her hide-and-seek skills.

Aylin has three brothers, and as she likes to say, "I have every kind of brother – an older brother, a twin brother, and a little brother." Parenting Aylin is a world apart from parenting all the "brothers." My oldest, Torin, was a breeze. He potty-trained himself, did what we asked without fuss, and bedtime was a cinch. When we had Torin, we thought, "Wow, this parenting thing isn't so hard." (Famous last words!)

As a mother of four, I adore each of my kids, but with more than one child, I quickly realized how different their needs can be. What works for one rarely works for all. Take breakfast, for example. In my early days of motherhood, I envisioned myself serving gourmet breakfasts like those found at bed and breakfasts: scrambled eggs, crispy bacon, homemade pumpkin bread, and freshly squeezed orange juice. Torin embraced this vision, but the dream ended when our twins arrived. Fourteen years later, we've learned that providing a buffet is the best way to ensure our kids even eat breakfast as they run out the door to catch the bus to school. In the mornings, we lay out all the cereal, yogurt, and fruit and step back, sipping our coffee while it's still hot.

Just as I had to adapt my parenting, I learned the same lesson as a teacher. I've been an educator for 20 years, starting as a high school English/language arts teacher. Initially, I taught the same way I'd been taught in high school – a syllabus based on novel studies, using the same reading list from my high school days. I lugged out cardboard boxes filled with *Of Mice and Men*, *Lord of the Flies*, and *Fahrenheit 451*. I assigned readings as homework, gave pop quizzes, and insisted on five-paragraph essays in blue or black ink on lined paper. I even taught that respect meant "Eyes and knees toward me" (I apologize to my former students!).

When I taught a class full of mythical "average" students like my oldest, Torin, this approach seemed fine. But then, things changed. Schools recognized the moral imperative of inclusion, particularly for historically excluded minorities and marginalized students. Inclusion was more than just a seat in the classroom; it meant creating a space where students felt welcome, had high expectations for success, and received the support they needed to learn.

Universal Design for Learning (UDL) is the framework that breaks down and removes the barriers preventing students from accessing their rightful place in a classroom community. It's where they can work toward clear goals, engage in meaningful learning experiences, and feel supported, celebrated, and like they belong. Fortunately, I taught in a school that valued inclusion and supported my journey into UDL. As my class grew more diverse, so did the options I offered for learning and sharing knowledge.

I realized that not one objective required every student to read a hard copy of a novel. My standards called for teaching how characters interacted within a text and how these interactions added depth to the story. Students could choose their own books – hard copies from the library, eBooks, or audiobooks. To share their learning, they could write responses or leverage emerging digital technologies like assistive and augmentative communication devices for responses. Going further, the standard didn't mandate writing; students could record videos, create multimedia artifacts, and collaborate to adapt their favorite texts into film projects. As students took ownership of these opportunities and tools, I had the chance to conference with them, create small, targeted intervention groups, and truly connect, learning what made each student extraordinary.

One of my main goals as a teacher was to know my students well enough that when I met their parents and families during Back to School Night, I could explain why our class would be incomplete without their child. Inclusion isn't just about placing students in a classroom; it's about creating an environment where they're welcomed, with high expectations to drive their success, and where they have what they need to learn. To do this, teachers need time to truly get to know each student, which is difficult in a one-size-fits-all classroom where they are the "sage on the stage."

Meeting the needs of every student was not something I could achieve alone. I was incredibly fortunate to work closely with special educators, school counselors, ELL specialists, school psychologists, families, and the students themselves. Collaborating, learning, and most importantly, listening prepared me to meet each child's needs in my classroom. I used to reassure parents of students who had previously been in substantially separate settings, "My classroom WILL be the least restrictive environment for your child because if there is a barrier that makes it too restrictive, we will eliminate it." I want all teachers to be confident and supported to say the same.

But the truth is, we're not quite there yet.

Today, as an educational consultant, I have the privilege of traveling worldwide and working with schools and districts committed to inclusion and UDL. Many of these systems face barriers that prevent them from providing the necessary professional learning, flexible curriculum, and tiered support systems that allow all students to be included with their peers while also accessing specific supports academically, behaviorally, socially, and emotionally. When students don't have these options, parents become frustrated, and understandably so. This frustration often stems from parents not recognizing the barriers teachers face due to a lack of systemic support, such as ongoing professional learning, collaboration time, and access to high-quality, flexible instructional materials. Parents may also feel frustrated that teachers may not yet have the capacity to meet their child's needs. This frustration and mistrust cycle ultimately affects the children we care about deeply.

But there's a better way – it's called working together. For students to succeed, adults must work together as well. We must understand where everyone is coming from, listen to each other, understand the barriers we face, and collectively work to overcome them. Ultimately, many passionate, dedicated individuals love and believe in our students, and the lack of structural and systemic support erodes our passion, hope, and belief in finding a better way.

Lori and Amanda reached out to me and asked me to read their book and I immediately fell in love. From the very first chapter, they captured both my Momma and my Teacher's hearts. They are incredibly vulnerable as they share their struggles and the barriers they've faced as educators, clinical professionals, and parents. Their stories highlight the moral imperative of this work and their research-based guidance provides us with evidence-based practices to start making these changes.

At the beginning of this foreword, I shared that having my amazing daughter required a change in my parenting style. Our life is now infinitely more beautiful, rewarding, and exciting because of her. The same is true in our schools and classrooms. Yes, including students with complex support needs requires changes – a shift in mindset, the development of new skills that demand flexibility, collaboration with families, and advocacy for systemic change. For far too long, we have served one-size-fits-all systems and this book is what our field needs to take another step forward.

I hope you love this book as much as I did and that it reminds you of the power of love, resistance, and change. And hopefully, within my career, I will see truly inclusive schools and places where all kids belong and thrive. And then, you can be sure I will jump out from my metaphorical clothing rack and scream, "We winned."

Acknowledgments

Words cannot adequately express the depth of our gratitude to the many individuals who have contributed to this journey. Writing this book has been an enlightening and enriching process and it would not have been possible without the support and encouragement of some truly remarkable people.

First and foremost, our test readers: Stephanie Kreatsoulas, Lusa Hung, Jackie Beardsley, Tanya Farrol, and Nicole Demos. Your invaluable insights, critical eyes, and honest feedback shaped this book in ways we couldn't have foreseen. You challenged us, cheered for us, and pushed us to strive for excellence. Thank you for your unwavering dedication and patience.

To our loving and ever-supportive husbands, Tam Ly and Michael Boll. Your faith in us and endless encouragement provided the backbone of this project. Your love and companionship have been a source of strength, comfort, and inspiration.

A heartfelt thank you to the rockstar Katie Novak, whose fierce advocacy in the field and generous spirit have been both a beacon and a helping hand to new authors like us. Your passion and leadership are awe inspiring and we are grateful for your influence and guidance.

We extend our deep appreciation to Elizabeth and her mother Catherine Blyth, and Laurence Audet Beaupre for opening up and allowing us to share their stories. Your contributions have added depth, authenticity, and heart to our work, helping us paint a vivid and true picture of the lives and experiences we're striving to represent.

A special acknowledgment to Jon Springer for your quote and advocacy for our neurodiverse children. Thank you to the International Self-Care Foundation for providing new language and structure for the self-care movement. We appreciate allowing us to utilize the Seven Pillars Graphic. Gratitude and appreciation are also in order for coming in and saving the day with your graphic skills, thanks Scott Lillis.

Last, but not least, we offer our profound gratitude to SENIA International for being the frontrunner in international schools in advocating for inclusion. A special shout out to April Remfrey and Andrea Lillis for your continued support throughout the process.

To all who have touched this project and our lives, thank you from the depths of our hearts. Your influence extends beyond these pages and has left an indelible mark on us both. We are forever grateful.

Introduction to *Navigating Special Education Relationships*

Conversation on a subway in Shanghai, China, in 2009:
This conversation below is between a psychologist and teacher (who happens to also be a parent of a child with special needs.)

Psychologist: Parents and teachers are so frustrating. I spend all this time creating programs and interventions that are highly effective in the research, but they just WON'T implement them. I don't understand. I only spend 3 hours a day with the students and the parents and teacher spend the other 21 hours with them. I can't make progress with them unless the parents and teacher do their part!

Teacher/Parent: I can totally see why you are frustrated. I know that when we received some recommendations from our psychologist, they seemed impossible to implement. I wonder what else is happening in that family's home, making it so difficult?

Psychologist: They come to me as the professional and pay for my opinion. Why can't they listen to my suggestions? They ask for my help yet don't want to do anything I suggest. It's especially frustrating because we know early intervention is key and don't want to waste precious time!

Teacher/Parent: I hear you, but I also know that as a teacher, I have 28 other students – also with their own strengths and challenges – so sometimes it can feel unreasonable to carry out those specific recommendations while balancing the needs of all the other students.

Psychologist: But what about the parents? They are the ones asking for my help and they spend the most time with their child.

Teacher/Parent: Easier said than done, my friend. Sometimes I just laugh at the list of recommendations given to us. We have so much going on that no one else knows about, like extreme lack of

	sleep, meltdowns, getting him to all the different therapies, and carrying out all those therapist recommendations. AND we have another child who is busy with her school demands and outside activities. It can feel insurmountable at times.
	You know who is frustrating me? My son's teacher and therapists. Aside from being his mother, I also need to be his case manager! I feel like a broken record, needing to repeat myself over and over to every member of his team. It's as if they don't communicate with one another.
Psychologist:	Yeah, it must be really challenging for parents. I didn't realize how much they are constantly juggling. Teachers and therapists should consider your feedback more and work on addressing some of the barriers parents have.
Teacher/Parent:	It's so weird being a teacher and a parent. There are many times when I think I know my student best and can't understand why the child's parent won't accept my thinking and other times when I put my parent hat on, I totally get it.
Psychologist:	Someone needs to write a book about how to navigate all these relationships.
Teacher/Parent:	Yes. It's so complicated. Someone really should.

And scene.

You may have guessed that the preceding conversation above between the authors. We met in Shanghai, China, in 2008 as directors of a school and clinic for students with special needs. Lori directed the school program and Amanda ran the clinic. We discussed various issues during our weekly meetings and noticed a common problem. There seemed to be conflict among staff and parents alike regarding the services provided to our students. These conflicts cause hurt feelings, negativity, wrong assumptions, disrespect, lack of trust, and a general sense of inauthenticity and tension in team meetings. We all felt this disjointedness (out of lockstep) but couldn't articulate the source of this issue at the time.

Upon reflection, we noticed a pattern. The conflict almost always stemmed from misunderstandings involving parents, teachers, and therapists and was tri directional. Any one of these three parties can misunderstand another.

This pattern of misunderstanding each other is a result of miscommunication. This observation was confirmed throughout our experiences over the past 25 years. Rarely is the "problem" a matter of *not* knowing what best practices are with working with students with special needs. The biggest problem lies in both communicating and building relationships among the team members. In other words, the problem is NOT that we don't know what works with this population of learners. The problem is that we **communicate ineffectively** in our collaborative teams.

The problem is NOT that we don't know what works with this population of learners. The problem is that we communicate ineffectively in our collaborative teams.

In addition to this breakdown in communication, we stumbled upon something else that seemed to make a bad problem worse. When unaddressed, our mental and physical health impacts us. HOW we show up each day as teachers, parents, and therapists plays a crucial role in how we interact with one another.

As a parent of a child with severe special needs, Lori was acutely aware of the stress and exhaustion parents experience. The stressors of daily life, extreme sleep deprivation, and inability to take care of her mental and physical health, compounded with a lack of empathy from some individuals working with her son, set the stage for mistrust, overwhelm, and miscommunication. While parents have a unique set of stressors, teachers and therapists also struggle with a similar set of problems.

The pattern that we've witnessed is that often in an attempt to prioritize our students, we deprioritize ourselves. In caring for others, we end up neglecting our self-care.

This book examines the two variables of RELATIONSHIPS (among care providers) and SELF-CARE, which we believe can interfere with our ability to optimally influence the individuals with whom we work. Recognizing and reckoning these two variables will negatively or positively impact all treatment efforts.

A bit about the authors

Lori comes to you as a mother and master's level special educator with over 25 years in the field. Lori, her husband Michael, and two children, Madi and Braden, spent 19 of those years in international schools around the globe. When Braden was five years old, he was diagnosed with profound autism and an intellectual developmental disability. This diagnosis led her family on a journey they never expected.

Braden is now 23, and Lori's family repatriated back to the United States in 2020.

Lori has walked the path that many families are just beginning and feels ready to advocate for not just the children with whom she's worked for over 25 years but their families, therapists, and teachers as well.

Amanda comes to you as a child psychologist with over 22 years of experience working with young people with various disabilities and a parent of a typically developing daughter. She began her career in the United States, moved to China, and back to the United States before going abroad again to Singapore. Amanda has worked in assessment and treatment in residential facilities, clinics, and home settings. She has focused her career on autism and development disorders and holds a PhD and Board Certification in Behavior Analysis.

Amanda feels strongly about helping families identify what's going on with their children and assisting them in making sense of things. Once diagnosed, her goal is to make families as informed as possible so that they can navigate their personal journeys with as much ease as possible.

A bit about the book

We divided this book into three sections: Discovering, Navigating, and Empowering. First, we outline the process of "Discovering" that you have or are working with an individual with special learning needs. Second, we outline methods of "Navigating" the waters of teaching/parenting/counseling the individual. Third, we outline strategies for "Empowering" all parties in the collaborative team. We examine this entire process of Discovering, Navigating, and Empowering through the lenses of parents, teachers, and therapists. We believe all individuals should

1 Understand the importance of relationships and self-care
2 Consider various perspectives
3 Work more collaboratively (e.g., "Collective Efficacy")

We believe we can foster more authentic communication and connections when addressing these three points. In the end, things improve not just for those individuals/families with whom we are working but for the entire team surrounding them.

Our hope and our promise to you as the reader is that you will feel seen and supported and that you gain some practical solutions to better facilitate collaboration or Collective Efficacy among all parties involved with special needs services. Ideally, you will experience a lot fewer headaches surrounding these relationships.

Notes

We understand that the terminology in this field is always changing. In an effort to be inclusive and use positive language, we have reconsidered the use of the term "special needs." Disability advocates argue that "special needs" are simply human needs, making the label unnecessary. We agree with this perspective. Emily Ladau, the author of *Demystifying Disability: What to Know, What to Say, and How to be an Ally*, suggests alternative terms such as "inclusive education," "accessible education," or "adaptive education" (2021). We also explored terms like "exceptional needs" or "exceptionally abled," but after consulting with Ladau, we realized that these terms often serve as euphemisms to avoid directly addressing disability, which is unfortunately stigmatized. Ladau points out that there is no universally accepted alternative term for special education (Ladau, 2021).

While we agree with Ladau's recommended terminology, we decided to use widely accepted terms like "individuals with special needs," "special needs," or "disability" to ensure that we reach a broader audience and avoid confusion for those who may not be familiar with these new terms. However, we strongly believe that individuals with disabilities are neurodiverse and offer unique perspectives that bring immense value to society.

We acknowledge that we have unintentionally overlooked a crucial member of our collaborative team: the individuals themselves. In all best practices, it is important to include the individual in the decision-making process when it is developmentally appropriate and the student feels comfortable participating.

Navigating Special Education Relationships is applicable to readers worldwide, regardless of their geographical location. While many of the authors' experiences have been in the international sector, the lessons and stories shared in this book are still relevant. We simply want to make it clear to readers that they may need to consider the context of public versus private settings instead of solely focusing on the international sector.

Although many of our stories reference autism spectrum disorders (ASD) due to the authors' expertise in this area, the themes, lessons, and practical suggestions can be applied to almost all categories of special needs.

Part I
Discovering

1 Collective Efficacy

Written by Dr. Ly

The following chapter is written by an educational professional and provides a comprehensive examination of the concept of "Collective Efficacy," focusing on its development and application within educational environments, specifically special education. It is intended for educators, researchers, and professionals working in the field of education, particularly those interested in enhancing collaboration and success within school settings. The detailed overview of the theory and its applications serves as a resource for those seeking to understand and apply these principles to improve student outcomes and collaboration among education teams.

When teams of educators believe they have the ability to make a difference, exciting things can happen in a school.

(Donohoo et al., 2018)

Remember the study from Stanford University in the 1970s that used Bobo dolls? It is the one where kids watch adults and peer models interact with those weighted dolls that spring back up after hitting them. Albert Bandura conducted this study. Interestingly, this is probably his most famous research study, yet he rarely gets noticed for another study with a more significant impact: the phenomena we now know as *Collective Efficacy*. In his early research, he noticed that a group's confidence in its abilities to be successful appeared to be associated with actual greater success. While he wasn't specifically examining educational settings, researchers discovered this phenomenon to be true across many domains. This is excellent news – something along the "power of positive thinking" – but more along the lines of powerful GROUP thinking. In essence, if a team of people believes that they are better able to overcome challenges and be successful by joining forces, they typically ARE successful (Bandura, 1997).

> *... powerful* group *thinking. In essence, if a team of people all believes that by joining forces, they are better able to overcome challenges and be successful, they typically ARE successful.*
> *—Albert Bandura*

Since the 1970s many additional researchers confirmed these results and saw similar patterns emerge from the data. In 2015 Kim and Shin showed that in a company when members of a team held strong positive beliefs about their capabilities, those beliefs proved to be true. This was evident in increased creativity and productivity.

In 1993, Bandura began noticing this phenomenon unfolding in a school setting. He observed that when educators (teachers, administrators, and faculty) combined forces, they more positively affected student outcomes. In his 1993 study, Bandura cited significantly higher levels of academic achievement, and later in 1997, he coined the term "Collective Efficacy." Donohoo, Hattie, and Eells (2018) adopted Bandura's definition as "a group's shared belief in its conjoint capability to organize and execute the courses of action required to produce given levels of attainment."

Since Banduras' initial discovery of a pattern of behavior and later coining Collective Efficacy in 1997, multiple other researchers started studying and publishing their work. By 2011, there was enough published research to aggregate the results and quantify what they found (meta-analysis). Rachel Eells authored this meta-analysis and noted another vital finding in school settings. The "beliefs teachers hold about **the ability of the school as a whole** are strongly and positively associated with student achievement across subject areas and in multiple locations [emphasis added]" (Eells, 2011). It is not enough to just believe in ourselves. We must ALSO believe in the system of support and our colleagues.

> *It is not enough to just believe in ourselves, we must also believe in the system of support and our colleagues as well.*

Researcher John Hattie joined the movement and is now considered one of the leaders in Collective Efficacy research. In 2016, Hattie made the strong statement that "Collective Efficacy [was] at the TOP of the list of factors that influence student achievement." By this time, we all knew it influenced achievement, but John Hattie made us aware that it is arguably the MOST important thing we can do to influence success with our students.

> *Collective Efficacy is arguably the most important thing we can do to influence success with our students.*

Dr. Hattie continued to aggregate all the data, studies, and information published on Collective Efficacy and reported his synthesis of over 1500 studies. This massive body of research showed another very powerful effect – "collective teacher efficacy is greater than three times more powerful and predictive of student achievement than socio-economic status" (Hattie and Zierer, 2018). Further, collective teacher efficacy is "more than three times more predictive of student achievement than student motivation and concentration, persistence, and engagement" (Hattie and Zierer, 2018). This is a huge finding for educators. The external variables of socio-economic status and parental involvement left educators frustrated. These variables were something teachers could do little about but were essential for student success or lack of success. The Collective Efficacy research findings demonstrate how school culture and a positive belief system MATTER MORE than any other preexisting barriers our students face. To give an example of just how powerful these results are – in Hattie's meta-analysis – Collective [teacher] Efficacy had an effect size of 1.57, where an "average" effect size is considered .40!

> *The collective efficacy research findings demonstrate how school culture and positive belief systems MATTER MORE than any other preexisting barriers our students face.*

Another area examined within Collective Efficacy research is the concept of school culture. Just like positive behavior supports influence the entire school's culture, so does Collective Efficacy. When educators, faculty, and administrators share a sense of the collective spirit, school cultures shift.

When Collective Efficacy is embedded in a school's culture, you will see educators' efforts supported and enhanced. It is empowering and collaborative. Educators lean into complex problems and reach out for assistance. In a school system that practices high-quality Collective Efficacy, faculty will dig deep, persist through challenges, and assume responsibility for student learning.

At a 2018 conference for school principals (LEAP Principal's conference), Hattie broke down the concept of Collective Efficacy into what it is and what it is not. Let's begin with what it is NOT. Collective Efficacy is not teachers simply getting together to discuss students or the curriculum or even being the cheerleader for students. It is not about a growth mindset or differentiated instruction. While those things all have a place and impact on learning, they are not the crux of the concept. Collective Efficacy IS hard work. It is getting together and understanding how we are going to impact students. It is about having difficult conversations. It is about understanding that teachers are the reason for student learning. By understanding the true meaning of the concept, that what we do has a profound impact on our students, we are better able to come to each discussion ready to engage purposely.

Hattie (2018) says that for groups to be successful with Collective Efficacy, they must do the following:

1 Plan for the discussion/create an agenda – state the goal of each meeting and stick with that goal throughout.
2 Monitor progress – determine how they will gauge that what they are doing is working (or not).
3 Actively listen – listen for understanding and repeat back for clarification.
4 Demonstrate empathy.
5 Have a leader who can moderate the discussion – this person ensures people take turns and actively participate.

A successful meeting is measured by recipients having equity in speaking time. Each individual feels listened to and empathized with, and listeners can demonstrate their understanding of what they heard.

Success lies in the critical nature of collaboration and the strength of believing that together, administrators, faculty, and students can accomplish great things. This is the power of collective efficacy.
—Donohoo, Hattie, and Eells

At this point, you may be wondering what any of this has to do with *Navigating Special Education Relationships*. We propose taking the proponents of school and teacher Collective Efficacy and extending it to our special education teams. These teams extend beyond the walls of the school building and into our homes and therapy centers. We aim to create effective collaborative teams by building the Collective Efficacy of our parents, teachers, and therapists, all with a common goal: to ensure the student's success at the core of our relationships.

Throughout this book, we use our stories and experiences and research from multiple sources to build upon the tenets of Collective Efficacy. We know that every single person on our team has the same goal, so how do we come together to ensure this? Viewing *Special Education Relationships* through the lens of Collective Efficacy, we assert that by believing in the capabilities of ourselves, others, and our students, we become a collaborative team. In doing so, we reach greater heights together than we ever could on our own.

We assert that by believing in the capabilities of ourselves, others, and our students, we become a collaborative team. In doing so we reach greater heights together than we ever could on our own.

Reflection Questions

1 **Understanding Collective Efficacy in Context**: How might the principles of Collective Efficacy be applied in your own team or community to foster success?
2 **The Power of Belief and Collaboration in Education**: Reflect on the statement that Collective Efficacy is "more than three times more powerful and predictive of student achievement than socio-economic status." What are the implications of this finding for educators, administrators, and policymakers? How can schools foster a culture that prioritizes Collective Efficacy, and what barriers might they face in doing so?
3 **Collective Efficacy and Special Education Relationships**: The text suggests extending the concept of Collective Efficacy to special education teams, including parents, teachers, and therapists. How might the principles of Collective Efficacy change the dynamics and effectiveness of special education collaborations? What strategies could be employed to build and sustain Collective Efficacy within these specialized teams, and what potential challenges need to be addressed?

2 Discovering a Disability

Sniffing Socks and an Autism Diagnosis

Written by Lori

The next chapter is written from a personal and emotive standpoint, as the author shares their first-hand experiences as a parent dealing with their son's early signs of autism and the challenges they faced in obtaining a diagnosis. The account is narrated with emotional depth, highlighting the confusion, isolation, and frustration that marked the family's journey. Other parents who may be facing similar challenges as well as educators, therapists, and professionals in the field of special education may benefit from the insights and empathy offered by the author's lived experience. Overall, the chapter serves as both a personal narrative and a plea for understanding and support for families navigating the complex world of autism diagnosis and intervention.

(Blog post first printed December 11, 2016, updated September 2021).

There was a time before Braden's diagnosis of profound autism and intellectual delay, and that time was incredibly difficult. We lived in Jakarta, Indonesia, and worked at an international school. Our daughter was happily attending preschool, playing with her friends, and loving life. She had quite an impressive vocabulary and just loved learning. Braden was much different. We watched him turn from a sweet and engaging baby into one who wouldn't look at us or engage. I remember watching Braden as he turned over his play truck when he was about 13 months old, lay down next to it, so his eye was next to the wheel, and simply spun the wheel repeatedly for over an hour. I remember being puzzled but didn't worry too much about it. Then, I noticed that he no longer turned his head when I called his name. He no longer smiled when I came into the room. He started having behaviors that were not like anything I'd seen my nephews, nieces, or friends' children do. Something was wrong with my son! The word "autism" entered my mind, but every time I brought it up to someone, they would brush it off and say, "No, Lori. I've seen children with autism before. Braden is so social. There's no way he has it." I tried to believe them.

My husband and I lived in a state of constant confusion. Braden and our daughter came from the same parents, pregnancies were normal, and they grew up in the same environment. So why did his sister talk so early? Where were Braden's words?

Braden started melting down in public, in the school parking lot, in the grocery store, and park. The judgment we received from people was too much to bear. People were constantly telling us how to be better parents, telling us we needed to discipline him, telling us we shouldn't allow him to behave that way. When they kicked us out of the public places because he was "too loud" or "scaring the other children," I couldn't say, "My son has autism," and then hope they'd understand. He didn't have a diagnosis. So, I just had to cry. And I cried a lot. I, too, was frustrated with him, his noise, and his behaviors. I knew something was wrong, but what was it?

Braden had daily meltdowns; he broke lamps, vases, and plates, screamed at the top of his lungs, kicked, bit, and pulled out his own and my hair. I was truly at a loss as to what to do. And since I was constantly living in crisis mode, I didn't have the time or energy to research it.

Due to a bombing in Bali (2002) and threat of terrorism in Jakarta, I took both kids to our home in Oregon while Mike stayed in Jakarta. We had planned to return to Jakarta once the threat disappeared, but life had other plans.

So, living as a single mother in crisis mode in Oregon, struggling each and every day, I had no idea what to do. Luckily, my husband's sister helped us. She researched and found out that Oregon had something called Child Find. As it turns out, Child Find is a mandate from the Individuals with Disabilities Education Act (IDEA) and is found in every state in America.

> Schools are required to locate, identify and evaluate all children with disabilities from birth through age 21. The Child Find mandate applies to all children who reside within a State, including children who attend private schools and public schools, highly mobile children, migrant children, homeless children, and children who are wards of the state.
> (State Eligibility, 20 U.S.C. 1412 (a)(3) 2015)

Making that phone call to Child Find was probably one of the hardest things I've ever had to do.

"Hello, my name is Lori Boll and ... I think ... I think (deep breath) something is wrong with my son."

Fast forward a few weeks. The woman from Child Find came to our home and observed Braden. Afterward, she sat me down and said that she saw a lot of symptoms of autism in Braden, and he would need further assessment. My parents came to visit that night. I had to tell them that the lady thought Braden might be autistic. "No ... he can't be," they said. Their only understanding of autism was the movie Rain Man, and this panicked them. I tried to help calm them down by saying, "It's okay. He will be okay. Autism is not a death sentence." And we know it is not! I tried to remain positive as I thought, "Well, I'm a teacher. Michael's a teacher. We've got this."

A few more weeks went by, and it was time for Braden's assessment. He was given the Autism Diagnostic Observation Schedule (ADOS).

The ADOS-2 is a widely used, semi-structured assessment tool that allows systematic and standardized evaluation of the presence of ASD symptoms. It includes five modules (Lord et al., 2012): the Toddler Module for children aged 12–30 months without phrase speech, Module 1 for children aged 31 months and older without phrase speech, Module 2 for children with phrase speech who are not verbally fluent, Module 3 for children and young adolescents with fluent language, and Module 4 for older adolescents and adults with fluent language. While insufficient on its own for a diagnosis, the ADOS-2 is considered the field's "gold standard" for collecting standardized and objective information about social communication skills, restricted interests, and repetitive behaviors (Maddox, 2021).

During this assessment, they asked Braden to do things like pretend he was at a birthday party, blow out a pretend birthday candle, and so on. They asked him to speak. He didn't. He did go to the window and say, "It's snowing outside." I honestly can't remember the rest. All I remember is this. My good friend came with me to the assessment because I was afraid I couldn't do it on my own. Michael was back in Jakarta finishing out his teaching contract. The people who gave the assessment gave us the results. I could barely focus. I was only listening for a diagnosis. But in the end, I never got one. So, I asked, "Does this mean he is not autistic?" From what I remember, they said that there wasn't enough evidence to say he was autistic and didn't score high enough on the scale or something like that. A good reminder for therapists is that *parents do not hear everything you tell them during an assessment review. They are stressed, worried, and listening for a diagnosis.*

We left. I asked my friend, "He's not autistic?"

She replied, "Nope, it doesn't look like he is."

That day I made the plane reservations to head back to Jakarta to be with Michael. Braden wasn't autistic. He must be okay. Right? I could go back to normal life.

Wrong.

We knew in our hearts that even if it wasn't autism, it was something, and we could no longer continue to teach overseas. There were no therapists in Jakarta, and we didn't feel like we had the skills to support him on our own. So, Mike picked up a teaching job in Denver, Colorado, and we moved to our new home.

Braden started attending a preschool program in our school district. He had a great teacher, friendly classmates, and some very helpful professionals, but it soon became apparent that Braden was an outlier. He was very loud, never played with any of the other children, didn't engage in conversation, and didn't participate in class. Child Find to the rescue. They once again came to our house. At first, they tried to tell us that since Braden didn't have a diagnosis of autism, then they couldn't put him into their special preschool autism program. Although he showed all the signs, he didn't have the diagnosis. Mike said something about going through "mediation," and suddenly, Braden was admitted into the program. Hey, we do what we have to do for our kids, right? Now, this is a good reminder for parents. School districts will not always do what is right for the child. Sadly, funding becomes a factor. Parents must be their child's advocate, and if they are unable to do that, they should find someone who can be that advocate for them.

Braden moved to a new preschool program with the most incredible group of specialists I've ever met. These professionals were the best in the business, and we are forever grateful for the hard work they put in with Braden and their constant communication with us.

After working with this group for two years, Braden still didn't have a diagnosis. None of them were willing to say he was autistic. Braden had tremendous skills in some areas and was very low in others. We needed a diagnosis, however, as kindergarten was looming. No diagnosis meant no special programming for him.

Enter Children's Hospital in Denver. Doctor McMonster (not her real last name) was the developmental pediatrician who saw us. We went into her office. She took off Braden's socks and smelled them. To this day, I still have no idea why she did this. She watched Braden for about ten minutes. He was in the windowsill repeating something over and over again (I can't remember what it was).

Suddenly, she looked over at the school psychologist who came with us to the evaluation and exclaimed, "And why haven't you people diagnosed him with autism? Isn't it obvious he has it?"

So yes, this is how we got Braden's diagnosis of autism.

He received this diagnosis at the age of five. We started noticing Braden was showing signs of a disability just after his first birthday. How could it possibly have taken this long? How could anyone in the world think that this would be an appropriate way to share a diagnosis with a family?

Believe it or not, we laugh about Diagnosis Day. For so long, we struggled and stressed and were afraid that Braden might be autistic, and in one crazy sentence, we were not-so-lovingly told that he was.

We are pleased that diagnoses are made for children on the spectrum at a much younger age now and that awareness campaigns have made it easier for people to recognize the early signs and symptoms. Children are diagnosed as early as 14 months of age. As everyone knows, early intervention is critical, so families benefit from this early diagnosis.

Sometimes I wonder why we accepted Dr. McMonster's diagnosis of autism, but I think we were just finally ready for it. We were somewhat relieved that we had a name for what was going on. Sometimes I wonder if the diagnosis is even correct. Braden isn't what you would call "classically autistic," but then again, is there such a thing? Does it even matter? I don't think so. He's getting the care and education he needs, and that is what matters in the end.

I don't hate Dr. McMonster. She told us what we needed to hear: our son was differently abled. I'm not bothered by the fact that she was so rude. I am bothered by the sock-sniffing though!

You may be wondering why I shared this story with you. The point is not for anyone to sympathize. It's more for readers to begin to understand that from the period of time when parents recognize there is something "not quite right" about their child's development to the time they finally receive a diagnosis is highly stressful. In our case, it took four stressful years to get an actual diagnosis.

Throughout this book, we refer to parental history. As educators and therapists, we may not know the struggles our families went through before we meet for the first time and we may come with our own assumptions as to how to best support the student.

Many parents won't be ready to accept their child's diagnosis, which can be very difficult for you. We suggest you ask parents about their discovering phase, acknowledge the struggles, and ask how you can support them moving forward. Most importantly, we ask that you believe the best in them and understand that they've already traveled a long, arduous road, even if their child is still young.

And whatever you do, don't start any meeting by smelling their child's socks [wink wink].

Reflection Questions

1 As teachers and therapists, how can we better understand and empathize with parents who are in the process of discovering and accepting a disability diagnosis for their child? What strategies can we implement to offer support and build trust during this challenging period?
2 The author mentioned that their child's diagnosis of autism took four stressful years to receive. How can early intervention and awareness campaigns play a crucial role in identifying disabilities at a younger age? How might this early identification positively impact the child and their family?
3 Reflect on the importance of effective communication when discussing a disability diagnosis with parents. What are some best practices for delivering this information sensitively, respectfully, and without adding unnecessary stress to the parents' experience?
4 The author mentioned that their child's diagnosis might not fit the "classical" definition of autism, but what truly matters is that the child is receiving the care and education they need. How can educators and therapists tailor their approaches to meet the unique needs of each child, even if they don't fit neatly into a specific diagnostic category? How can we promote a more inclusive and flexible understanding of disabilities in our practices?

3 Discovering the Diagnosis Dilemma
To Label or Not

Written by Dr. Ly

The subsequent chapter is written from a psychologist's perspective, focusing on the intricate issue of labeling a child with a diagnosis in an educational context. It navigates the decision-making process of obtaining a diagnostic assessment, considering various stakeholders including parents, teachers, and pediatricians. The author discusses reasons for and against labeling, the choice between public and private evaluations, and implications for the child's future, including considerations of insurance coverage and costs. It is intended for families dealing with the diagnostic process, educators, and healthcare professionals and the chapter concludes with detailed tips and resources.

One area that is often at the root of many disagreements between parents, teachers, and therapists is whether or not to label a student. Parents express a concern that they don't want their children to be labeled and have that label follow them throughout their educational careers. Teachers often push for a label as they believe it helps create a roadmap to best support the child. As a psychologist, I often counsel parents on whether they should proceed with a formal evaluation, which leads to a diagnosis. Before going into the actual process of conducting an assessment, I think it is essential to talk about WHY you would even consider having an assessment conducted on a student at all. Another consideration is WHERE to conduct the evaluation: pediatrician, psychology clinic, or school setting. I examine the why, the where, and the benefits of each.

Should you get a formal diagnosis for your student? I wish I had a definitive answer, but the most honest and accurate answer is that it depends.

In graduate school, during a supervision meeting, a professor and I had a conversation about diagnosing in the clinical setting. When I gave my assessment of the diagnosis of a case I was working on, the professor asked a fundamental question: "Why?" I was confused. "What do you mean, why? Isn't this what we're supposed to be doing?" He clarified, "What is the treatment? If the diagnosis does not inform treatment, don't give the diagnosis."

Diagnosis in a clinical setting is imperfect as we don't always have the luxury of being able to directly inform treatment beyond our recommendations. That professor was trying to teach that it is not enough to simply label kids—we need to evaluate problems in a thorough and comprehensive way and not merely put a label on them. What we DO with that label matters. Rather than just labeling a kid, we only want to assess them if we know that assessment would lead to better-informed treatment. In essence—use assessment to inform treatment.

Assessment/diagnosis is only meaningful if we use that information to inform treatment! Labeling for the sake of labeling needs to go by the wayside.

> *Assessment/diagnosis is only meaningful if we use that information to inform treatment! Labeling for the sake of labeling needs to go by the wayside.*

Why should you conduct an assessment at all? The simplest, straightforward answer is that parents usually notice when something is "off," or something is "wrong" and seek guidance and assistance. Usually, if this is the first child in a family, they may delay getting help if they do not notice because they have no point of reference. The first child is typically unfamiliar territory for most new parents. They do not have any older siblings to say, "Child number two is not doing what child number one was doing, so maybe we should get some input on that." Often, most people do not realize something needs further investigation until they enter school for the first time. It is then that the parent can start comparing them to other same-aged peers.

Pediatrician

Many pediatricians are generalists and can detect a wide variety of common conditions, which serve most children's needs incredibly well. Occasionally, however, you get a pediatrician who is not well-versed in developmental delays or autism spectrum disorder (ASD). They won't always see the signs early enough to guide and direct families most appropriately. As a parent, if you have a valid concern and your doctor says "wait and see" or "they'll grow out of it," this may signify limits to their area of expertise. This lack of awareness of their limits to their competence is concerning because the pediatrician is often the only line of defense against detecting early childhood conditions before the child enters school. Additionally, when you consider what we know about early intervention services, the literature tells us – much like many conditions in adulthood – that the earlier you detect a problem, the better the outcome or prognosis is. So, early intervention is vital in most cases and you do not want to waste any valuable time.

Interestingly enough, an article entitled *Grandma knows best: Family structure and age of diagnosis of autism spectrum disorders* claims that those children who had frequent interactions with grandparents and older siblings were more likely to be diagnosed at a younger age (Sicherman et al., 2017). In fact, the authors found frequent interactions with a grandmother reduced the age of ASD diagnosis by 5.18 months and frequent interactions with a grandfather reduced the age of diagnosis by 3.78 months. The other significant finding about the relationship between those closest to the individual who notice the warning signs of those later diagnosed with ASD is that of the household with older siblings. The presence of older siblings (when the youngest child in question has ASD) reduces the age of diagnosis by 9.5–10 months. The authors suggest that perhaps the older children "serve as a reference point" in aiding parents in discerning whether the younger child is "on target" developmentally.

Psychology Clinic

It is a personal decision whether it is best to do a public-school or a private evaluation. When guiding parents on which is better for their child, I ask them, "who do you want to own the information" or "who do you want to own the report generated from this evaluation?" If the parent does not mind that the school owns the information and that the data generated from the report is part of the child's cumulative record, then perhaps public-school evaluation is the best decision. If a parent is unsure how the report will be used or wants to own the information, then a private evaluation is the right decision for that family.

Often, in an international setting, I recommend getting a private evaluation. There is no guarantee how the report will be used. If a school ascribes to old-school ideology and uses the information to limit the child or deny access to a student, this is a reason to have a private evaluation. Suppose a school ascribes to a new-school ideology and uses the information to help communicate the child's needs and to adapt teaching to meet those needs. In that case, a public evaluation is appropriate.

The private sector exists throughout the world but is quite common in the expatriate arena. Internationally you have people from their home countries living elsewhere. These individuals do not have a public-school option per se, so they send their children to private international schools. These schools are often world class and are typically incredibly good at what they do. But these schools are not regulated by any federal laws requiring that they must provide services to children with special needs, so often, they do not. Since most expatriate kids move schools often, the report must move with the child to use as a tool to advocate for what they need. Without understanding how schools will use the information generated from the diagnostic evaluation, I generally advise parents to own the information or choose the private option.

If a private evaluation is preferred, the cost deserves a bit of commentary.

Cost

Yes, the cost is expensive (an average of 2,000–4,500 USD), as it is an extensive, time-consuming process. For me, it typically takes 8–16 hours of direct assessment time, then another 20 hours of scoring, case formulation, and report writing, so nearly 28–36 hours of work for one student. The cost alone is prohibitive; however, we wanted to highlight why it is expensive, how to increase the likelihood of getting it covered by your private insurance, and make a case that it may be worth the investment.

Insurance Coverage

I have worked with A LOT of insurance providers. There is a wide variety of terms and a huge gap in what is and is not covered. Typically, insurance providers love to use "medically necessary" or "medical necessity." IF the diagnosis in question is considered a "medical condition" and if the treatment is of "medical necessity," THEN they *may* cover it. Not very promising, eh?

I have discovered a few ways to increase the likelihood of getting covered. The best way is for you (the consumer) to educate yourself on your insurance policy. I can almost hear the groans from this side of the book. There are two main types of insurance providers in the United States alone: self-funded and fully funded insurance plans. The difference is who pays for the policy. Very large corporations typically fund their own insurance plans, as it is more cost effective. For example, Amazon and Microsoft will hire an insurance provider such as Blue Cross Blue Shield but then pay for it themselves, thus providing a Blue Cross Blue Shield self-funded plan, funded by Microsoft or Amazon. However, fully funded plans are typically purchased directly from the insurance carrier, so United Health Care is fully funding the plan. Many smaller employers opt for this, as it is more cost-effective. As of 2022, in the United States, it is becoming increasingly more likely to get funding for services (assessment, treatment) of various special needs conditions; however, MOST of the legislation applies exclusively to fully funded health care plans. You see the gaping hole, right?

Self-funded insurance plans are exempt from most legislation, so they typically will not cover services. That said, there is a handful of "woke" self-funded policies that will cover services, but it depends on your individual plan.

I once worked for a family living in Houston, Texas. Their employer, a large oil company, provided their insurance. Thus, it was a self-funded plan. The family had three older children and then tried for one more. Surprisingly, they didn't have just one. They had triplets. All three were diagnosed as severely impacted on the autism spectrum before their third birthday. When I met them, the family was doing everything right and struggling to get through each day safely. They needed help and needed help fast. I did not hesitate to begin working with the family in their home. I figured that we would deal with insurance later. Once we made the insurance claims, no surprise, they declined everything. The part I was NOT prepared for is that the reason for the decline was a complete fabrication. Yeah, did you know that they can do that? I was so angry and righteous (yes, I was fresh out of school), so I advised the mom to put her metaphorical boxing gloves on and we were going to fight for their right to get services.

Three rounds of appeals later, I had a phone call with the Chief Medical Officer of a large national insurer. No matter what evidence I brought forth, they stated, "No, there is not enough evidence for applied behavior analysis to warrant it as medically necessary." ARGH! I was furious, as I brought an arsenal of data and literature spanning decades showing just that: a strong evidence basis for the efficacy of applied behavior analysis (ABA) to be extremely helpful, especially for kids like the triplets! I tried explaining the importance of the *quality* of research. Tier 1 peer-reviewed journal articles are considered the gold standard, not—like he was showing me—an internally published PDF article by that insurance company falsely claiming that there was not strong enough evidence. I presented data from their parent organization (e.g., not just the self-funded branch in Texas), quoting their Chief Medical Officer. They correctly claimed that ABA was evidence-based and more cost-effective than paying for long-term residential treatment facilities! At the end of the day, the insurance policy was self-funded, so it did not matter if we were in the right or not. They had the right to deny it. Not cool.

After leaving Houston, I transferred this family's care to another excellent service provider who informed me that she took the torch from me and ended up successfully getting the services.

How can families increase the likelihood of getting insurance to cover assessment/treatment?

- Read and understand the individual policy.
- If possible, change insurance providers to get a policy covering mental/behavioral health.
- Learn what your insurance company considers behavioral/mental health vs. medical. (Some insurance companies classify ASD as neurological, e.g., medical, and some classify it as behavioral, e.g., mental/behavioral health). The distinction can make all the difference.
- Call the insurance company or your human resources department for an explanation of what is and is not covered.
- Only see qualified providers. Again, the insurance company outlines this. For example, with new federal legislation (in the USA) there is an increase in coverage for ASD; however, it must be by a qualified person. For ABA, a board-certified behavior analyst must deliver the program. And therein is the self-funded loophole.
- Know the Current Procedural Terminology™ (CPT™) codes that are and are not covered. Many insurance companies cover psychological assessments.

The following are CPT™ codes to familiarize yourself with for psychological assessment and another set for ABA treatment. The list is not exhaustive, but something to give as a starting point to ask the insurance provider or human resources manager what the policy does and does not cover.

Psychological Assessment CPT™
- 90791 Psychiatric Diagnostic Evaluation without Medical
- 96130 Psychological Testing by a physician or other qualified health provider
- 96132 Neuropsychological Testing conducted by a physician or other QHP

ABA CPT™
- 97151 Adaptive Behavior Assessment conducted by a physician or QHP
- 97152 Adaptive Behavior Assessment conducted by a technician
- 97153 Adaptive Behavior Treatment

In conclusion, the dialogue surrounding the diagnosis of a child in the educational setting is complex and multifaceted. It encompasses the perspectives of parents, teachers, and psychologists, each carrying their unique concerns and interests. As a psychologist and teacher, I have navigated the intricacies of these relationships, working to bridge the gap of understanding and foster a collaborative approach. The decision to seek a formal diagnosis for a child depends on numerous factors, including the child's unique needs, the intent behind the label, and the potential to enhance treatment. Furthermore, the choice of assessment venue—be it a pediatrician's office, a psychology clinic, or a school setting—holds its unique set of implications. The quest for a diagnosis should be driven not by a desire to label but by an intent to provide the best possible care for the child. Above all, this process should always prioritize the child's well-being and future prospects. A diagnosis may be costly and time consuming, but it is an investment with the potential for a lifetime of dividends. It allows us to understand the child more fully, to plan the most appropriate course of action, and to advocate effectively for their needs.

Reflection Questions
1. **Perspectives and Priorities**: Dr. Ly emphasized the differing perspectives of parents, teachers, and psychologists concerning the diagnosis of students. Reflect on how each group might prioritize the needs and long-term outcomes of the child differently. What are the key motivators for each group and how do they shape their viewpoints on diagnosis and labeling?
2. **Value of Assessment and Diagnosis**: Given Dr. Ly's assertion that "Assessment/diagnosis is only meaningful if we use that information to inform treatment," how do you feel about the current system's approach to diagnosis? Do you think there are instances where children might be labeled without clear treatment paths and if so, what implications does this have for the child's future?

3 **Early Intervention and Detection**: Dr. Ly mentioned the importance of early intervention and how it leads to better outcomes. How might the roles of family members, particularly grandparents and older siblings, be amplified in the early detection process based on the study cited? How can society better leverage these familial relationships to improve early detection?
4 **Insurance and Accessibility**: Dr. Ly highlighted the challenges of obtaining insurance coverage for assessments and treatments. Reflect on how these financial and bureaucratic hurdles might impact a family's decision to pursue a diagnosis or treatment. In what ways can the system be improved to ensure that every child has access to the care they need?

4 Discovering Complications With the Diagnosis Process
The Gatekeeper Problem

Written by Dr. Ly

The next chapter focuses on the issue of "gatekeepers" in the field of special needs diagnosis and is described from a psychologist's perspective. The author addresses the challenges in obtaining timely evaluations and interventions due to a scarcity of qualified professionals and the resulting delays. The chapter also highlights the challenges faced by school professionals and emphasizes the qualities necessary for a good diagnostician. Professionals working in special education or healthcare (such as diagnosticians, therapists, and educators) as well as parents and caregivers of children with special needs may benefit from understanding this issue. The chapter aims to shed light on the system's intricacies and offers guidance on understanding and navigating the diagnosis process, with an emphasis on collaboration and advocacy for the child's needs.

We find ourselves in unfamiliar territory where insurance companies and third-party funding sources have begun to provide coverage for individuals with special needs; however, they require a formal diagnosis conducted by certain qualified professionals. These key professionals are then viewed as "gatekeepers" to access services. There is a scarcity of qualified professionals, resulting in lengthy delays in getting access to evaluations and, in turn, interventions.

The gatekeeper problem is not as significant in the public-school sector but still exists. Often, the issue in the public school system is that the designated professional in the school setting has too large of a caseload to have the luxury of spending any significant amount of time with the student.

What makes a good diagnostician? Consider this

Diagnosis and comprehensive evaluation, when appropriately used, can be an enormous tool to help us understand what is going on with a student. It helps identify strengths and weaknesses and uses this data to help get our students back on track. The reports generated from these diagnostic evaluations help communicate a cluster of symptoms so that we can adapt our teaching, therapies, and instruction to help our students be as successful as they can.

The best-case scenario is when reports are used in this fashion. There are several reasons that, despite our best intentions, there is a breakdown in how diagnostic evaluations are obtained (the process) and used (outcome). However, I thought it was important to highlight that reports are not inherently bad and can serve as a tool for getting our students the help they need to remove barriers to learning. Deep breath ...

How do we get all the good parts of diagnostic assessments without all the bad?

Good Diagnosticians

1 Uncover the history of the problem. What's been done. What's worked. Back and forth between caregivers, students, and diagnosticians.
2 Administer a thorough battery. Cast a wide net. Rule in or out. Consider multiple sources.
3 Ensure family understands the write-up. Allow for questions.
4 Provide research-based recommendations. Consider the whole child.
5 Be available for follow-up.

A good diagnostician will take the time to walk parents through the often long report (most are between 20 and 30 pages). When I conduct my report presentation, I like to take it step by step so they can go through the same process of uncovering and identifying why their child is struggling in specific ways. It is almost like telling a story. Often, I can see the practically visceral desire of most parents to want to skip to the end and just tell them what the diagnosis is and what to do about it, but I think that is a mistake. You miss the big picture. You miss the buildup. You miss the formulation. A good diagnostician takes the time to explain the report, allows for questions, and ensures that the family leaves with a solid understanding of the report.

Let's flashback to Braden's diagnosis story. Remember, Lori couldn't hear anything during the report presentation because she was hyper focused on listening for a diagnosis for her son. Despite the psychologist's point of view that the "story builds up to the diagnosis," the parent's point of view is "please just tell me the diagnosis, then we can discuss how we arrived there." This fundamental difference in point of view is a perfect example of some of the misalignment between the two parties.

At the end of the report, there should be a list of recommendations. All good diagnosticians will include research-based recommendations informed by the individual student's profile. Additionally, it should include the whole student. In other words, we utilize their strengths and don't overfocus on their weaknesses.

Finally, all good diagnosticians will make themselves available for follow-up. This process is a doozy; thus, parents will not be able to come up with questions on the spot. They will inevitably need time to process things. A good diagnostician acknowledges this and will allow them the space and time they need to process and gladly assist the family throughout their journey.

How do you know if a diagnostician has done their job? The family walks away with a firm grasp of the report and a better understanding of their child. The single most important thing that families need to understand is that they are their child's best advocate. They are the ones who need to understand the contents of the report. They can relay that information to any future persons involved in their child's education and care. They will be the only constant throughout their child's life, so they need to be able to understand what support to get their child after the point of a diagnosis.

Navigating the labyrinth of diagnosis and professional gatekeeping may seem daunting; nonetheless, understanding that the diagnostic process can serve as an empowering tool is vital. As parents and teachers, you play an instrumental role in advocating for your students' needs. It's essential to recognize that while professional diagnosticians are crucial, they are part of a broader system where your role is fundamental. As educators, our ultimate goal is to optimize the learning environment to best fit each child's unique profile. Thus, understanding, engaging, and effectively utilizing the process of diagnosis becomes critical. Remember, the diagnostic process isn't merely a means to access resources but a pathway to understanding our children better, using their strengths to compensate for their weaknesses, and tailoring instruction to help them thrive. When well applied, this complex journey can shape a transformative story – a story that, albeit challenging, will ultimately illuminate the path forward for our students and their lifelong learning journey.

Reflection Questions

1 **The "Gatekeeper Problem"** Reflecting on the "gatekeeper" challenge described in the chapter, how might the current system be restructured to expedite the evaluation process, ensuring that children receive timely interventions without compromising the quality of assessments?
2 **Value and Challenges of Diagnostic Evaluations**: Consider the balance between the benefits and challenges of diagnostic evaluations. How can educators, parents, and therapists ensure that the diagnostic process remains a tool for understanding and assisting students rather than becoming a hindrance or source of stress?
3 **Understanding the Diagnostic Report**: The chapter highlights the importance of parents thoroughly understanding the diagnostic report. If you were an educator or therapist, how might you help bridge the gap between the clinical language of a report and a parent's desire to know the direct implications for their child's learning and development?
4 **Role of Diagnosticians, Parents, and Educators**: Delving into the complexities of the diagnostic process, how can parents and educators collaborate more effectively with diagnosticians to ensure a holistic understanding of the child? Additionally, considering the story of Braden and Lori, what strategies could professionals employ to align their approach more closely with the needs and emotions of the families they serve?

5 Discovering Prevalence Rates and Screening Tools

Written by Dr. Ly

The next chapter provides essential background information about the current prevalence rates and introduces a few screening tools. It's designed to be a resource for teachers, parents, and professionals working in this field.

Warning – unlike our anecdotal stories, the information presented in the next few chapters may elicit yawning. Although a bit boring and dry, we still thought it was important to include.

This chapter presents background information, prevalence rates, and the additional components involved in a comprehensive diagnostic workup to shed light on what happens behind the scenes or how a report is created. I hope that this demystifies the process so that parents, teachers, and therapists gain a better understanding of these reports. Research tells us that when teams have a common goal and learn to trust, respect, and communicate one another's points of view it sets the stage for collaborative teams. Gaining an understanding of all parties' perspectives during this process sets the stage for HOW to create a culture of Collective Efficacy. When a team of people believes that they are better able to overcome challenges and be successful by joining forces, that is Collective Efficacy.

In the world of child psychology, psychopathology can include but is not limited to anything that affects a child's ability to learn in terms of:

- Academic Behaviors (i.e., reading, writing, and mathematics)
- Psychological/Mental Health Conditions (Internalizing – i.e., depression, anxiety or Externalizing – ADHD or conduct problems)
- Cognitive Deficits (i.e., low IQ or intellectual disability).

Prevalence Rates

According to the Center for Disease Control and Prevention (CDC), 1 in 6 U.S. children aged 2–8 years (17.4%) has a diagnosed mental, behavioral, or developmental disorder (March 2022). Table 5.1 shows prevalence rates for four common diagnoses.

DOI: 10.4324/9781032634357-7

Table 5.1 Prevalence Rates of Select Special Needs Categories

Condition	Prevalence	Comments
Autism Spectrum Disorders (ASD) (CDC, 2020)	One in 36	4x as prevalent among boys as among girls
Attention-Deficit/ Hyperactivity Disorder (ADHD) (DSM-5-TR, 2022, p. 72)	7.2% of children worldwide	Male:female difference 2:1
Specific Learning Disabilities – Reading, Writing, and/or Mathematics (DSM-5-TR, p. 82)	5–15% of school-aged children	Diagnosed differently in schools vs. clinical settings
Intellectual Disability (DSM-5-TR, p. 44)	Overall, 1%; slightly higher in lower income countries at 1.6%	Must show both low IQ and deficient adaptive functioning

According to the National Center for Educational Statistics, in 2019–20, 7.3 million students aged 3–21 received special education services under the Individuals with Disabilities Education Act (IDEA), or 14 percent of all public-school students. Among students receiving special education services, the most common category of disability (33 percent) was specific learning disabilities.

Screening Tools

Typically, throughout the course of early childhood, parents take their children to pediatricians for various "well check" or preventive care appointments. These (usually yearly) visits are the first line of defense against determining if everything is going well or not. The pediatrician or developmental specialist, nurse, or whoever you see for the child's regular check-ups measures height and weight and whether they are meeting their developmental milestones.

One of the most widely used developmental screeners is the Modified Checklist for Autism in Toddlers, Revised with Follow up™ (MCHAT-R/F™, 2009). Anyone can download and use this checklist for FREE – https://mchatscreen.com/.

Drs. Robbins, Fein, and Barton developed a simple screener administered as part of a comprehensive well-child visit intended for children aged 16–30 months. The screener is very simple, consists of only 20 yes/no questions and takes approximately five minutes to administer. When administered to children universally (e.g., through well-child visits) and during the intended age range, it is extremely good at identifying the presence of autism. Most kids will be negative for risk of ASD; however, those screened as "at-risk" will take the second part of the now two-part checklist (Revised AND Follow Up). Of those "at-risk" kiddos (scoring at or greater than 2–3), the MCHAT-R/F™ showed a 94.6% risk of having a developmental delay.

The primary benefit of the screener is that it is highly sensitive, meaning it is likely to OVER flag "at-risk" children, which has actually led to decreasing the age at which a child is diagnosed and ultimately gives them earlier access to intervention (Robins et al., 2014). The follow-up portion of the screener for those kids who are flagged "at-risk" takes an additional 5–10 minutes and should be conducted by a professional. The first portion of the screener does not require any special training. It is free and should be used as the first step during universal screeners in the developmental period. For reference purposes, the outcome of the MCHAT-R/F™ will give the user a number that indicates the level of risk the individual is at having autism spectrum disorder (Low Risk 0–2; Medium Risk 3–7; High Risk 8–20) (Robins et al., 2009).

Spread the word – universally screen for ASD using FREE screener – Modified Checklist for Autism in Toddlers Revised and Follow Up™ (2009) available here – https://mchatscreen.com/.

Please see the CDC website for a comprehensive list of developmental milestones in an easy-to-use format. If everything is going well and as per the developmental milestones, your child is developing as expected. However, suppose a child does *not* hit these developmental milestones. In that case, it is regarded as a red flag and the pediatrician will either investigate further or advise what to do at that stage. Unless your pediatrician is well versed on every single childhood condition that exists, you will not always have those warning signs until a later time when you do have someone more familiar with something such as autism.

To screen for concerns relating to attention deficit/hyperactivity (e.g., problems with executive functioning), there are a few good screeners, including Conners, Behavior Rating Inventory of Executive Functions (BRIEF), and Child Behavior Checklist (CBCL).

To screen for concerns relating to specific learning disabilities, schools should be conducting universal screening using curriculum-based measures as part of a multi-tiered system of supports (MTSS, formerly known as Response to Intervention or RTI) across reading, writing, and math. They may include something like Dynamic Indicators of Basic Early Literacy Skills (e.g., DIBELS).

To screen for intellectual ability or cognitive functioning concerns, your primary care provider should be monitoring developmental milestones; however, if you still have concerns, go to the checklists on child development on the CDC website. When armed with data, you'll often find that your provider may take your concerns more seriously and set the stage for a more in-depth discussion.

The Developmental Assessment of Young Children – 2nd edition (DAYC-2) is a great tool to screen for several early childhood concerns from birth to 5 years 11 months and was last updated in 2012. The DAYC-2 measures developmental levels in the following domains: cognition, social-emotional development, physical development, communication, and adaptive behavior.

As we conclude this comprehensive exploration of prevalence rates and screening tools, it is my hope that the complex behind-the-scenes processes involved in psychological diagnostics have been demystified for parents, teachers, and therapists alike. Although the data and details can seem overwhelming, remember that this information is a crucial part of building a strong, cohesive team around each child. When we understand these processes and can interpret the numbers, we are better equipped to advocate for our children and students. Moreover, this knowledge fosters an environment of Collective Efficacy, where we believe in our collective ability to overcome challenges and succeed. While screening tools provide essential early insights, the role they play is just the beginning. The path to understanding each child's unique learning profile and finding the best strategies to support them is a continuous journey. Be it ASD, ADHD, or specific learning disabilities, our primary goal is to use these tools not just for classification, but to open doors for individualized instruction and timely intervention. And remember, despite the complexity, the essence of our mission is simple: to champion the best possible outcomes for our children.

Reflection Questions

1 **Understanding Prevalence**: Reflect on the prevalence rates presented in the chapter. Were any of the statistics surprising to you? How do these prevalence rates change or shape your perspective on the need for screening and early interventions in schools and clinics?
2 **The Importance of Screening Tools**: How do you think the early screening tools like the MCHAT-R/F™ can potentially change a child's life trajectory? How does the early identification of potential developmental concerns contribute to better outcomes for children?
3 **Collaborative Efficacy**: Dr. Ly mentioned the concept of "Collective Efficacy," wherein people believe that by joining forces, they can overcome challenges. Reflect on your experiences or observations. Can you think of a time when a team of professionals, parents, and educators effectively collaborated to support a child's needs? What were the outcomes, and what factors contributed to the success of that collaboration?
4 **Personal Advocacy and Screenings**: Considering the numerous screening tools and resources provided in the chapter, how might parents and educators become better advocates for children's needs? How can parents and educators ensure they are informed and proactive in recognizing the early signs of developmental or learning concerns in children?

6 Discovering the Diagnostic Assessment Process

Written by Dr. Ly

The subsequent chapter is an informative guide detailing a best practice procedure for performing comprehensive diagnostic evaluations. While various methods exist to conduct high-quality comprehensive assessments, this chapter specifically describes how one psychologist approaches the process. It is designed to assist parents, teachers, fellow psychologists, and other professionals in understanding how to both create and interpret these reports.

When I conduct my diagnostic assessments, my general rule of thumb is that I screen for a wide variety of conditions or behaviors. I include academic behaviors, cognitive abilities (e.g., Intelligence Quotient aka IQ), and psychological disorders, including behavioral conditions (i.e., grief, trauma, anxiety, depression). Best practices in psychology warrant that I examine behaviors across time, so I do not just take one data point but instead gather data across multiple different time samples. I also collect information from a wide variety of informants or sources of information. Utilizing multiple sources of information is probably the most important thing you can do to get an accurate perception of what is going on with a child. Suppose you only see a child once in a clinical setting. What happens if they do not exhibit the behavior in question or if they start exhibiting new behaviors because they are nervous, tired, sick, or hungry? Taking just one data point (as often is the case in doctor/clinic settings) does not allow for an accurate sample of behavior; thus, it is considered best practice to take several instances of behavior across time. Additionally, getting the most accurate example of a child's behavior requires us to gather information from ALL of those involved in the child's life or who play an essential role in a child's life.

When I first see parents, we often have a conversation where I state that I wish evaluating psychological conditions was more like medicine. Medical testing is usually more straightforward, where you can do a blood test and know with high certainty what is occurring. Unfortunately, that does not exist in psychology. In the absence of this, "best practice" in clinical and school psychology is to gather information across time, from to multiple people, and in various settings. Once you have done this and the information points toward the same thing, you have a higher degree of confidence in accurately identifying the underlying condition. When all the data points to the same criteria, that is how you have the highest degree of certainty regarding what conclusions you draw versus what you can rule out as the explanation for the behavior(s) in question.

Humans are complex, and issues are rarely black and white. I would even go out on a limb and say *nothing* is black and white. We are always in the gray. Many variables interplay in determining why we behave the way we do. This method of clinical "best practice" ensures that we are the most confident in our decisions by providing information that either converges or diverges (points toward or points away from) the conclusions that we draw.

When I think about assessment in terms of school or clinical evaluation of various childhood conditions, I think about a few different things. When I evaluate a child, I screen for a wide variety of conditions because you never know what may be a primary or a secondary condition. For example, after evaluating a child, you conclude they have a specific learning disability. However, you realize later that they recently moved or that their parents have just gotten a divorce. They are not exhibiting an authentic specific learning disability but what is better explained as a behavioral or psychological condition. It is best practice to screen for a wide variety of conditions to get a better, more complete picture of what is going on with an individual or child.

Steps Involved in Evaluating a Child/Adolescent
- Developmental History – History of the Problem
- Interview
- Test: Academic, Cognitive, Psychological
- Synthesize Data/Information
- Draw Data-Based Conclusions
- Write Report
- Make Appropriate Recommendations

While casting a wide net when examining a child for the first time, the first step is to interview the caregiver and the child depending on their development/age/verbal abilities. The interview allows me to determine what is going on with the child/presenting problem from the caregiver's perspective. During the interview, I include child development, history of the problem, and what the family has previously tried (what has or has not worked) to gather an up-to-date perception (Figures 6.1 and 6.2).

When I screen, I examine the following areas: academic behaviors, cognitive ability, and psychological conditions. When examining academic behaviors (depending on the child's age), I investigate the areas of reading, writing, and math. I am looking to see how they perform relative to benchmarks or age

36 *Discovering*

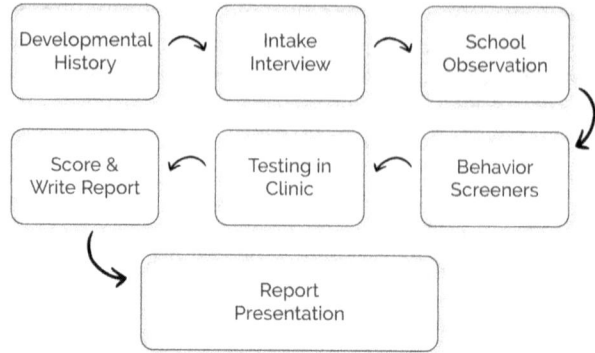

Figure 6.1 Flow Chart Dr. Ly Comprehensive Diagnostic Assessment

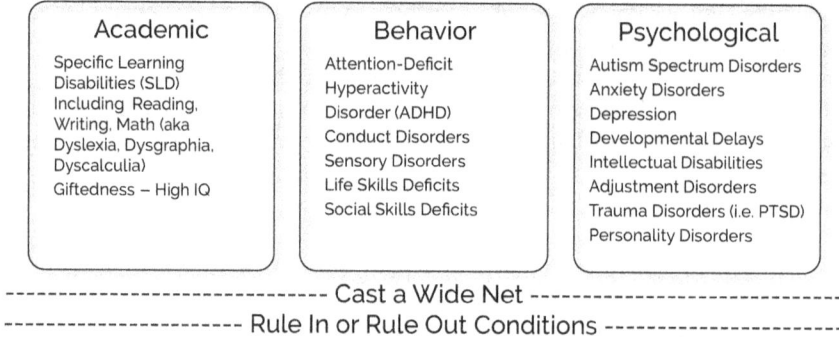

Figure 6.2 Cast a Wide Net to Rule In or Out

norms. If the child is too young, this would not be relevant, but this is an excellent place to start if they exhibit an academic problem to determine if it is chronic or acute (Figure 6.3).

When screening psychological conditions, I look at various behaviors and will solicit input from multiple informants. A child never exists in a vacuum or isolation. I mean that there are many individuals involved in a child's life, including parents (e.g., Mom, Dad, stepparents, caregivers, guardians, grandparents), teachers or educators, clinicians, physicians or nurses, and therapists (Figure 6.4).

Different therapists involved may include speech and language therapists or pathologists, occupational therapists, physical therapists, and a whole host of others. When working with a child, it is essential to gather information from these individuals so that you can poll the entire group of people involved in the child's life to get the most accurate perception of what is currently going on. Gathering information from multiple informants is especially important when the child is functionally nonverbal. For example, a child may be exhibiting

Discovering the Diagnostic Assessment Process 37

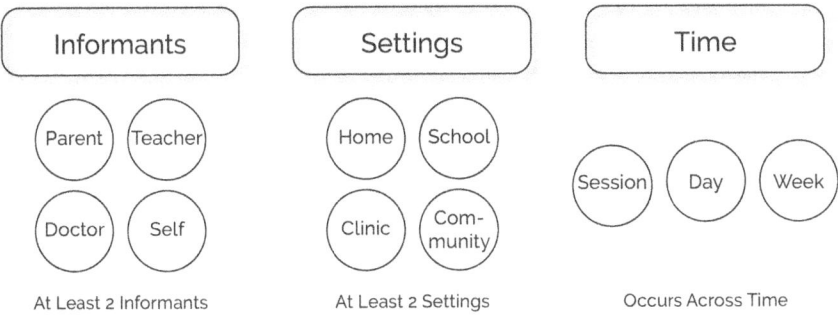

Figure 6.3 Guideline for Best Practice in Assessment

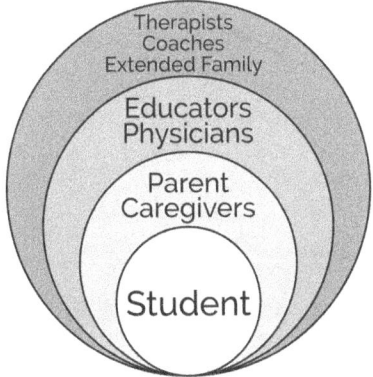

Figure 6.4 Sources of Informants

certain behaviors only in one environment but not in another and it is crucial to understand why that is. Likewise, if a child exhibits behavior across all settings and among all caregivers, it is also essential to know that information. The more people (informants), environments, and persistence across time, the more confident we can be with our diagnosis. However, best practices dictate that the minimum requirement for ruling in or diagnosing a condition requires evidence that the behavior(s) in question occurs according to multiple people (informants), across multiple settings, AND across time. You must have proof of all three of these. The more data pointing to the same thing, the more confident we are in our clinical decision. See Figures 6.5 to 6.7.

Behavioral conditions can include conduct problems, aberrant behaviors, or social behaviors exhibiting areas of excess or deficit. Whether a behavior is problematic or not usually depends on whether it is a behavior you *want to occur versus you do not wish to happen*. A behavior may be problematic when exhibited in excess if it is a behavior you do *not* want to see. For example, a child is constantly biting their nails such that it interferes with their ability to

38 *Discovering*

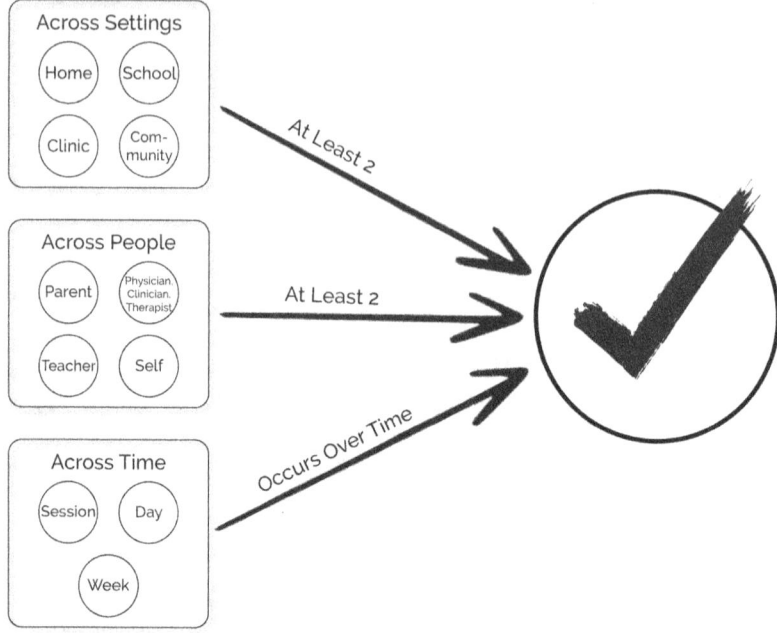

Figure 6.5 Diagnosis Confirmed

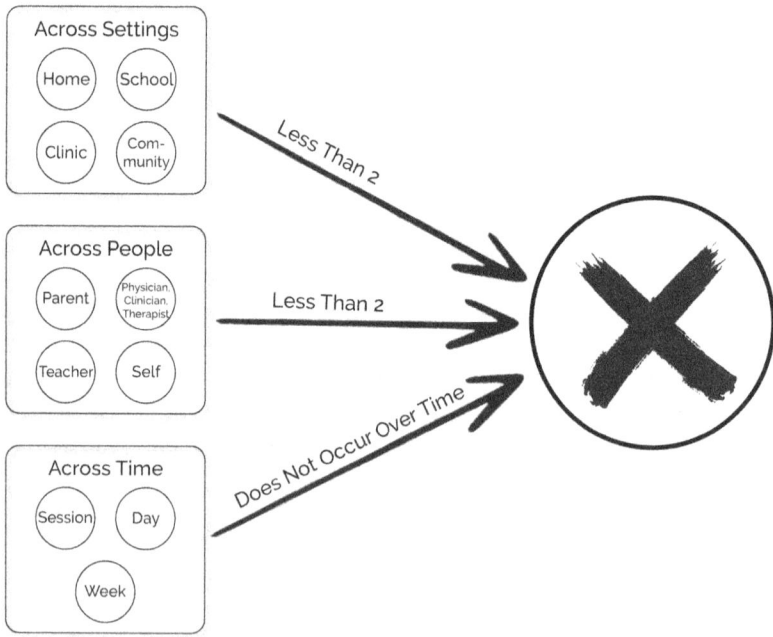

Figure 6.6 Diagnosis Contradicted

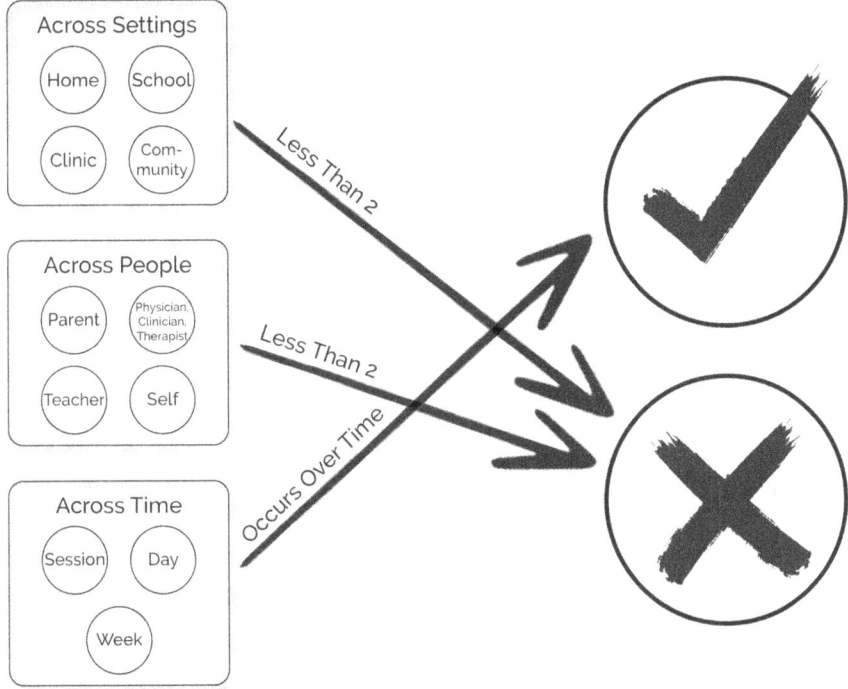

Figure 6.7 Diagnosis Inconclusive

learn. Nail-biting is an example of a behavior excess and is considered problematic. Additionally, there are problems of behavioral deficit when an individual is NOT exhibiting behaviors that you *want* to see, for example, when a child is not currently engaging in prosocial behavior or behaviors to assist them in interacting with their peers, such as cooperation or turn-taking.

An IQ score should NEVER be used in isolation to identify or diagnose conditions, but instead used as part of a larger work up.

Cognitive testing is also known as testing intelligence or IQ. The history of cognitive tests dates back to the early 1900s. The first test was created by a French psychologist, Alfred Binet (The Binet-Simon Scale later became the

Stanford Binet Test of Intelligence). These early versions of intelligence testing were used to identify and sort individuals based on "intelligence." Not surprisingly, IQ tests were brought into military and police institutions and eventually schools. In the beginning, cognitive testing was purely a test that reflected an individual's innate "abilities" and was a true reflection of one's intellect. Later, researchers uncovered that IQ tests held many biases. For example, they tested only certain known areas of intelligence, had cultural bias', and were very heavily verbally loaded. Basically, if you are very verbal, you will score much higher. If you are nonverbal or a non-native speaker of the test language, you will perform more poorly. Of course, there are "nonverbal IQ tests," but even then, the construct of IQ requires a lot of verbal language to evaluate.

Why test cognitive "abilities"? However, imperfect it may be, it is currently our best tool for evaluating whether intellectual delays are present. As with most things in psychology, it is not a perfect system but one that we can use as a data point or as a piece of evidence. I would not recommend taking stock in a solid number. Still, when I discuss IQ, I describe it as a range in which we are confident the individual will function that is stable across their lifetime (after approximately six years of age). For example, if someone has an IQ of 111, I prefer to focus on the range 105–116, where I will describe this individual's IQ by stating, "we are 95% confident that his true IQ score is between 105–116" across their lifetime. For ease of communication, most people say the 111 number, but you would state it in terms of the confidence interval to be more precise. A confidence interval gives a range in which we are confident that the "true" score lies. Again, I advise not to hyper-focus on IQ but use it as a tool to screen for cognitive deficits/delays or higher cognitive abilities (as in intellectually gifted).

The key takeaway from screening for cognitive "abilities" is to determine if the individual is at, above, or below where we would expect (e.g., 85–115) and screen for further information. The normative data suggests that a standard score (adjusted to compare against other same-aged individuals) of 100 is considered average with a standard deviation of +/− 15. A score between 85 and 115 is considered "average," with much above or below that as above or below average. Individuals with an intellectual disability (formerly known as mental retardation) score ≤70 IQ (or two standard deviations below the mean). In contrast, individuals in the gifted range typically have an IQ of ≥130 (this is two standard deviations above the mean from grade 2 onwards; below grade 2 needs to score three standard deviations above the mean or 145+ given that IQ is not as stable before age six). An IQ score should never be used in isolation to identify or diagnose conditions but instead be used as part of a more extensive workup (Figures 6.8 to 6.12).

Screening for psychological conditions should occur from birth throughout childhood. It is imperative in early childhood to understand a child's development via developmental screeners so that you know whether a child is exhibiting developmental delays that can lean more toward autism spectrum disorders or other delays of development (i.e., intellectual abilities). Later, you also want

Discovering the Diagnostic Assessment Process 41

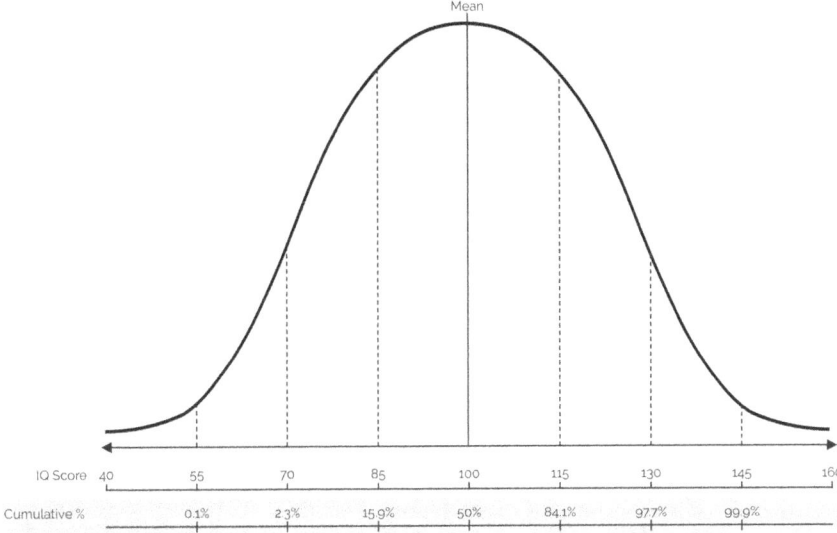

Figure 6.8 Standard Normal Curve

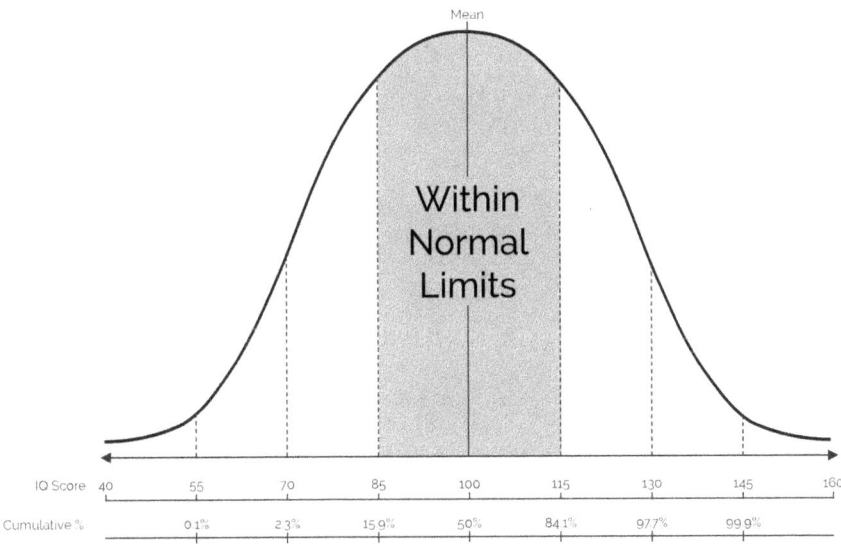

Figure 6.9 Cognitive Abilities Within the Normal Range

42 *Discovering*

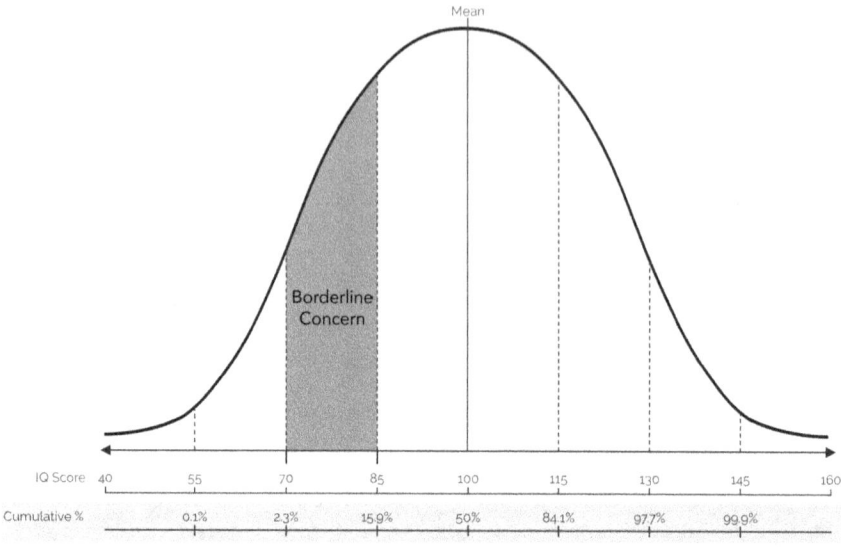

Figure 6.10 Cognitive Abilities Within the Borderline Clinically Significant Range

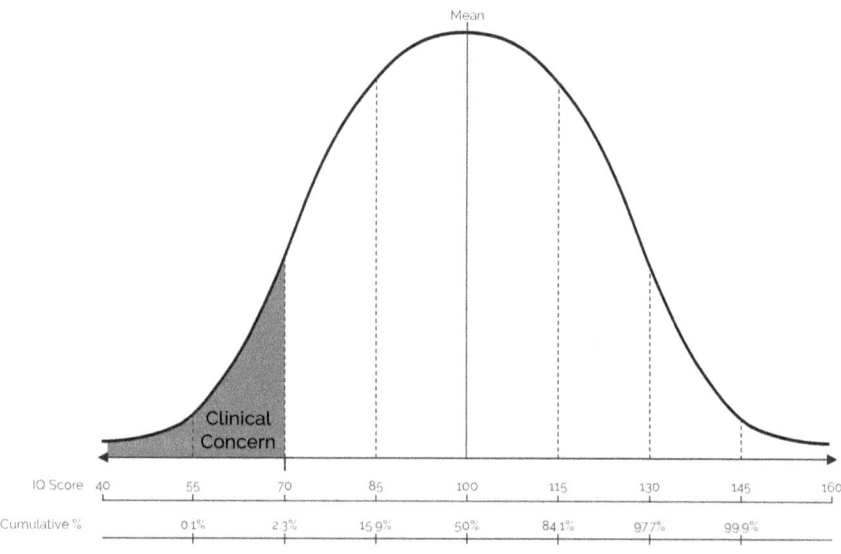

Figure 6.11 Cognitive Abilities Significantly Below the Mean and of Clinical Concern

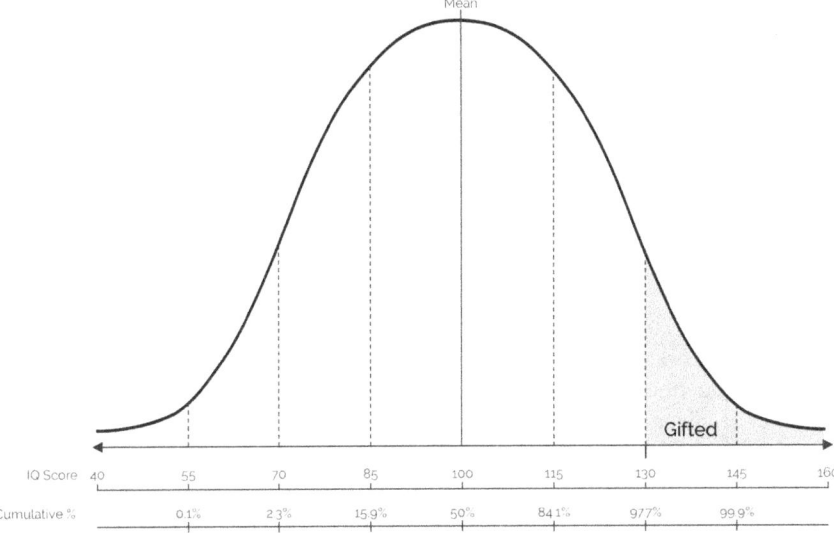

Figure 6.12 Cognitive Abilities Significantly Above the Mean aka Giftedness

to screen for internalizing and externalizing conditions to understand better what may also be co-occurring with a child. For example, screening for internalizing conditions (depression and anxiety) and externalizing conditions (attention deficit–hyperactivity disorder (ADHD)) or various conduct problems may also be co-occurring and need additional examination.

Once you "cast a wide net," you start to formulate a clinical opinion about what is going on with a child to determine an underlying condition or even simply understand the child's strengths and weaknesses. It is also vital to examine whether you think the condition in question is occurring because the child *cannot* do them versus whether they *will not*. I call this "can't do vs. won't do." What I mean by this is that the child can perform something versus if the child is willing (or often unwilling) to perform something. For example, is the child just choosing not to read, or can the child not read? There are ways to evaluate this, although sometimes it is not always so simple to tell the difference. Over time, and by gathering enough data from enough people familiar with the child, you can get a pretty good understanding of their "I can't do something versus I won't do something."

Public School Setting

Current best practices for public-school evaluations dictate that they are conducted through a multi-tiered system of support framework or MTSS. MTSS includes three tiers of increasing intensity of instruction, intervention, and support to identify specific learning needs. According to the Center on

Multi-Tiered System of Supports (2021), there are three essential components of this framework:

1 Screening
2 Progress Monitoring
3 Data-Based Decision Making

We will elaborate on the details of MTSS in the Informational Section later.

In conclusion, it's clear that the process of diagnostic assessment in psychology involves a thoughtful, meticulous, and thorough approach. Understanding a child's behaviors, cognitive abilities, and psychological conditions requires multiple data points, taken across time and informed by diverse sources, including caregivers, educators, and various therapists. This process is akin to casting a wide net – an approach that allows for a more accurate, nuanced perception of the child. In psychology, unlike in medical testing, there's no single definitive test that can provide answers with high certainty. Therefore, our "best practice" hinges on gathering information across time, from multiple people and in various settings. This multidimensional approach aids in formulating accurate diagnoses, considering the many variables that influence human behavior. From academic and cognitive assessments to screenings for psychological conditions, the evaluation process is designed to provide a comprehensive understanding of a child's strengths, weaknesses, and the underlying factors contributing to their behavior. In the end, the aim is to offer the most precise and well-rounded interpretation of the child's psychological condition and guide them toward the most suitable interventions and support structures.

Reflection Questions

1 **Reflection on the Complexity of Human Behavior**: Dr. Ly emphasizes the intricacy of human behavior, stating that people exist in the "gray" rather than in black and white. Reflect on your experiences or observations. Can you recall an instance where an individual's behavior was misinterpreted due to oversimplification or failing to consider multiple factors? How might a comprehensive diagnostic assessment have provided clarity?
2 **Assessment vs. Medical Testing**: The chapter highlights the distinction between diagnostic assessments in psychology and medical testing. Why is it vital to gather information from multiple sources, settings, and over time when assessing psychological conditions, unlike medical tests which might provide clear-cut results? How does this difference shape your perspective on mental health assessments?
3 **IQ Testing and Its Limitations**: Dr. Ly delves into the history and limitations of IQ testing, emphasizing that it should not be used in isolation. Reflect on societal perceptions of IQ and intelligence. How might cultural biases and the verbally loaded nature of many IQ tests affect certain populations?

What are the dangers of relying solely on an IQ score to make determinations about an individual's capabilities?

4 **The Role of Context in Behavior Interpretation**: The chapter introduces the concept of "can't do vs. won't do" to determine the root cause of a child's behavior. Consider a situation where a child's behavior might be misconstrued as defiance or unwillingness, but upon closer inspection, it's due to an inability or lack of knowledge. How can understanding this distinction influence the interventions or support provided to a child? How can professionals ensure they are making accurate determinations between these two scenarios?

7 Discovering the Diagnostic Process in School Settings

Multi-Tiered System of Supports (MTSS)

Written by Dr. Ly

The following chapter is an informative guide that explains the multi-tiered system of supports (MTSS) process. Its purpose is to assist both current and future teachers in implementing the latest best practices, and it also serves as a valuable resource for parents and other professionals working in schools.

A framework to support the early identification of students with learning and behavioral challenges, called multi-tiered system of supports (MTSS), is built on the groundwork of Response to Intervention (RTI). MTSS was built on the foundations of RTI and Positive Behavior Intervention Systems (PBIS) and extends the work of RTI in that it addresses both academics and behavior, whereas RTI was concerned solely with academics. Multitiered generally refers to three tiers that correspond to different levels of intervention support (https://mtss4success.org/, 2021). The M and T focus on the multitiered component but arguably the *most important* component of MTSS is the SS or System of Support. This system level application is typically the most challenging aspect of implementing MTSS in schools and districts. For now, let's lay the groundwork and get our MTSS bearings.

Tier 1, or universal/schoolwide support and instruction, is provided to all students, and most students (approximately 75–90 percent) respond well to this support. Tier 2 supports are more specialized interventions that meet the needs of the 5–15 percent of students who do not respond effectively to Tier 1. Tier 3 supports are more intensive, individualized interventions that typically meet the needs of the 3–5 percent of students who do not respond effectively to Tier 1 or 2 (Burns et al., 2016). These percentages are considered standard for implementing a multitiered framework but do vary. The MTSS framework includes processes for screening all students, providing tiered instruction and intervention support, and monitoring students' progress. MTSS is typically associated with general education and providing evidence-based programs to all students (Zumeta Edmonds, 2016). Response to Intervention (RTI) is a multitiered framework to address problems early for students at risk for poor learning outcomes. Schools identify struggling learners through universal screening and provide multiple tiers of evidence-based instruction and interventions. Identification is

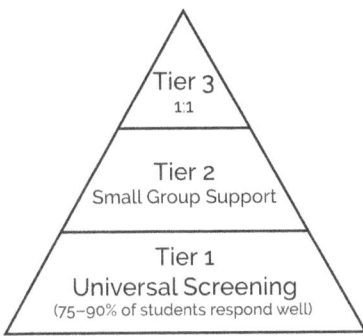

Figure 7.1 Multi-Tiered System of Supports (MTSS)

accomplished by 1) monitoring student progress, 2) adjusting the intensity and nature of those interventions depending on a student's responsiveness, and 3) as indicated, identifying students with learning disabilities or other disabilities according to state and district guidelines (Center on Response to Intervention & National Center on Intensive Intervention, 2014). Specific MTSS/RTI practices describe precise actions that educators interpret in the same way and that support implementing a practice as expected by a state.

MTSS provides a method of early identification and intervention that can help struggling students catch up with their peers. MTSS uses three tiers of support to assist all students at various levels. Please see Figure 7.1 for a visual representation of MTSS.

Tier 1: Primary Support

High-Quality Classroom Instruction

At Tier 1, all students receive high-quality, research-based instruction provided by qualified personnel. Schools universally screen students on a regular basis in reading, writing, and mathematics (side note: I would love to see screening for mental health too, but that's another book). MOST kids will score at grade level for reading, writing, and math (usually 85% of all kids) and will continue to receive their education in their current setting. Those who do not (usually around 15% of kids) will progress to Tier 2.

Tier 2: Secondary Support

Small-Group Instruction

Tier 2 takes the 15% or so of children who did not respond well to the regular curriculum and receive additional small group interventions. The groups are more intensive than regular curriculum teaching due to the lower student-teacher ratio. After this 6–8 weeks of intervention, another percentage of students will acquire the skills they were initially not getting at the Tier 1 level while other students may need to continue to receive Tier 2 support or may need more intensive Tier 3 support.

Tier 3: Tertiary Support

One-to-One (1:1)

Even after implementing Tiers 1 and 2, some students may continue to have significant challenges that do not respond to the interventions and support delivered in Tier 1 or Tier 2. Tier 3 gives these students individualized support and can include assistance from outside agencies, such as behavioral counselors or other therapists.

MTSS tiers help schools organize the levels of support contingent on the intensity of the interventions needed so that students receive necessary instruction, support, and interventions based on their own needs.

MTSS has evolved the way we think about special education placement insofar as we no longer simply refer-test-place students in the special classroom setting. Instead, we progress all students through the MTSS and only students who do not adequately respond well to Tiers 1 and 2 will advance to the highest intensity of intervention at Tier 3. At Tier 3, the individual will receive the highest level of individualized support (https://mtss4success.org/, 2021). This model helps eliminate the need to place students in segregated classrooms by meeting the students where they are in terms of the need for support. Many students formerly identified as needing "special education" who respond to Tiers 1 and 2 of MTSS no longer need the higher intensity support. This structure allows students to receive the minimum level of support necessary to achieve the required skills. Using MTSS is how all specific learning disabilities (reading, writing, math) should be evaluated and treated in a school setting.

There is a fantastic resource for all things MTSS–related—how-to, what it is, implementation, progress monitoring, and access to evidence-based interventions. See the Center for Multi-Tiered System of Support at the American Institute for Research at the following website: https://mtss4success.org/

Reflection Questions

1. **Understanding the Basis of MTSS**: The chapter mentions that MTSS builds on the groundwork of Response to Intervention (RTI) and Positive Behavior Intervention Systems (PBIS). Reflect on the relationship between these systems. How does the foundational knowledge of RTI and PBIS enhance your understanding of MTSS?
2. **Analyzing the Tiers**: Each tier in the MTSS has a specific function and addresses different needs. Considering the described percentages of students who typically need each tier's support, why is it important for schools to

have such a structured tiered approach? How might this system affect the stigma around needing additional academic or behavioral support?
3 **Application in Real-Life Scenarios**: Imagine you are a teacher observing a student who seems to struggle in the traditional classroom setting. Using the MTSS framework, describe how you would approach the situation to provide the student with appropriate support. What steps would you take to ensure the student receives the necessary interventions?
4 **Rethinking Special Education Placement**: The chapter discusses how MTSS has changed the perspective on special education placement. Reflect on the implications of progressing all students through the MTSS before making decisions about special education placement. How might this change in approach benefit students, teachers, and the broader educational system?

8 Discovering Concerns and Fears
Supporting General Education Teachers

Written by Lori

The next chapter is by a learning support teacher who has firsthand experience with inclusion in general education classrooms. The author offers insights and shares personal stories to illustrate the challenges and misconceptions related to including students with special needs in typical classrooms. It is intended for general education teachers, special education teachers, parents, therapists, and anyone involved in the educational system who might be interested in or responsible for supporting inclusive education. The chapter aims to advocate for better training and support for teachers in inclusive practices, as well as fostering a more accepting and empathetic educational environment for all students.

"I'm not trained to work with a child with special learning needs. Why are they putting him in *my* classroom? They should be put into Sue's classroom. She's more equipped to handle it."

If I had a dollar for every time someone said something like this to me, I'd be rich! Okay, not rich, but at least it would pay for a nice night out for dinner and a movie.

Why do some teachers say this? What are they feeling? That's easy to answer. FEAR. What do we do about this? Well, that's not as easy.

I worked as a paraprofessional while earning my master's degree in special education. During that time, I worked closely with a fourth-grade student, Zeke. Zeke experienced autism spectrum disorder and cerebral palsy, which impacted his speech and physical ability. Zeke's cognitive ability was very high, but poor fine motor skills made it so Zeke could not write. However, he could verbally answer any question. Zeke spoke loudly and it took practice to understand his verbalizations. It was clear that Zeke was brilliant when he shared his insights and answered questions.

Unfortunately, his general education teacher didn't think so. She clearly disliked having Zeke in her classroom. She often rolled her eyes when he spoke. Her impatience showed with each and every interaction. In general, she directed all her words to me. "Please tell him to write his name on his paper." Why didn't she just speak to Zeke directly?

This teacher often told him "No" and frequently asked me, as a paraprofessional, to take him out of the room as he was "disturbing the other students." I was new to the community and the school. So, I did as she asked. I'm still angry with myself about this fact.

First of all, Zeke did NOT disturb his classmates. In fact, his classmates adored him. They tried to include him in their working groups and games at recess. This teacher? SHE was disturbed by Zeke's differences. And she let it show. Zeke preferred time in the classroom with his peers. He liked them. However, it soon became clear to him that he was not welcome.

In hindsight, I should have refused to take Zeke out of the classroom. However, as a paraprofessional, this was not what I felt comfortable doing. I feared I would lose my job for not listening to this teacher. I wish I would have had the guts just to say, "Zeke is not disturbing his classmates. He is disturbing you because you are uncomfortable with teaching a student with a disability." This teacher **feared** my student. She **feared** his disability. Overall, she **feared** judgment from her colleagues for her inability to teach him.

This teacher feared my student. She feared his disability. Overall, she feared judgment from her colleagues for her inability to teach him.

Luckily, I believe this teacher is the exception and not the rule. The majority of teachers do not fear a child or a disability. However, they worry they won't be able to teach that child, which fills them with fear.

While I am immensely frustrated with the response, "I'm not trained for this," I realize they are right. Most teachers lack sufficient training to work with students who require additional support. A 2007 study stated that general educators reported taking 1.5 courses or fewer focused on inclusion or special education in their teacher preparation courses. Meanwhile, special educator candidates take an average of 11 (Mader, 2017).

With an increase in inclusive practices worldwide, the expectation is that general education teachers must work with various learning needs. With seemingly a bazillion diagnosable disabilities, this proves overwhelming for many who may think, "I've never heard of this syndrome. How can I possibly teach someone with it?" or "I don't know how to work with a child with dyslexia. I'm not a special educator."

When I look back to my teacher preparation program in the nineties, I had **zero** courses that helped me prepare to teach individuals experiencing a disability. Yes, **zero**. Dyslexia, autism, and executive functioning skills were not even present in my vocabulary upon graduation. I remember precisely **one** short lecture on effective classroom management. Differentiated instruction was never covered, as the goal was for us to teach the students in the middle, leaving out our twice-exceptional learners and students with learning needs.

While training has improved since the 2007 study, I challenge that it is *still* not enough. I recently presented at our local community college to a large group of early childhood teachers. I prepared two workshop proposals: one on executive functioning skills and the other on autism spectrum disorder. When I submitted these proposals, I thought, "No one will sign up for these. Everyone knows about them already." To my surprise, the conference approved both submissions. And after each presentation, multiple attendees approached to tell me this was all new learning for them. I was honestly shocked. New learning? Why shouldn't ALL teaching candidates learn about executive functioning and autism spectrum disorder? Everyone has some executive function challenge. Further, with 1 in 44 individuals diagnosed on the autism spectrum, every educator must be well versed on the topic.

So, if teachers are ill prepared to work with our students, what does this mean for those students? It means that teachers cannot help students develop executive functioning skills such as planning, organization, and time management if they don't even know how to identify these skills. It means that scores of teachers have students in their classrooms who are on the autism spectrum yet do not have the skills to reach and teach them. That isn't very comforting. Most importantly, it illustrates that many teachers do not hold the fundamental belief that all children want to learn or can learn.

Why are our teachers inadequately prepared to include students with disabilities? Perhaps that's for another book at another time. What can we do about it?

Make Inclusion a School or District-Wide Priority

Poor teacher training programs cannot be an excuse for one to decide they will not teach all students who enter their classroom. To combat this, schools and school districts must prioritize inclusive education. They must create an inclusion belief system and policy that is clearly defined and found on their website. They must hire educators who share in their belief system that all children can learn and have the right to learn in the least restrictive environment (LRE). Schools and districts must support their educators by providing them with professional development opportunities focused on disability education and inclusive practices. Schools need to work with teachers opposed to helping all learners and set up a plan with benchmarks and expectations for improvement. Should no progress occur after the intensive intervention with the teacher, the teacher must be fired. Does this sound harsh? Maybe, but for inclusion to be successful, every stakeholder dedicates time and effort to their understanding of the different learners who walk into their classroom each school year. If teachers are unwilling to change for the sake of their students, they are the people who need consequences, not the students.

Let me put this another way. In my prior example, the teacher should have been asked to leave the classroom, not Zeke.

> *[Regarding inclusion as a priority] If teachers are unwilling to change for the sake of their students, they are the people who need consequences, not the students.*

Build an Inclusive Belief System

So how can general educators, learning support teachers, therapists, and teachers work together, build our collective efficacy, and ensure all our learners are successful?

I'm not going to lie here. As a learning support teacher, I often judged general educators when they claimed they could not educate a student. I learned, however, that judging is not only wrong; it serves little purpose and prolongs the process of inclusion buy-in.

To prepare general educators for a student's arrival, I now do the following:

1 Prepare an IEP at a glance
2 Build-in co-planning/check-in time
3 Gently educate the teacher on the concept of Universal Design for Learning
4 Listen and empathize when the teacher vents and try to gain perspective

IEP at a Glance

As you read in Dr. Ly's chapter on assessment and report writing, reports are long and sometimes as extensive as 45 pages. Teachers do not have the time to read the information and process it. So, we need to summarize it for them in one easy-to-read page. An IEP at a glance is not new. Learning support teachers or IEP case managers have been doing this for years. Here is a sample (Figure 8.1).

54 *Discovering*

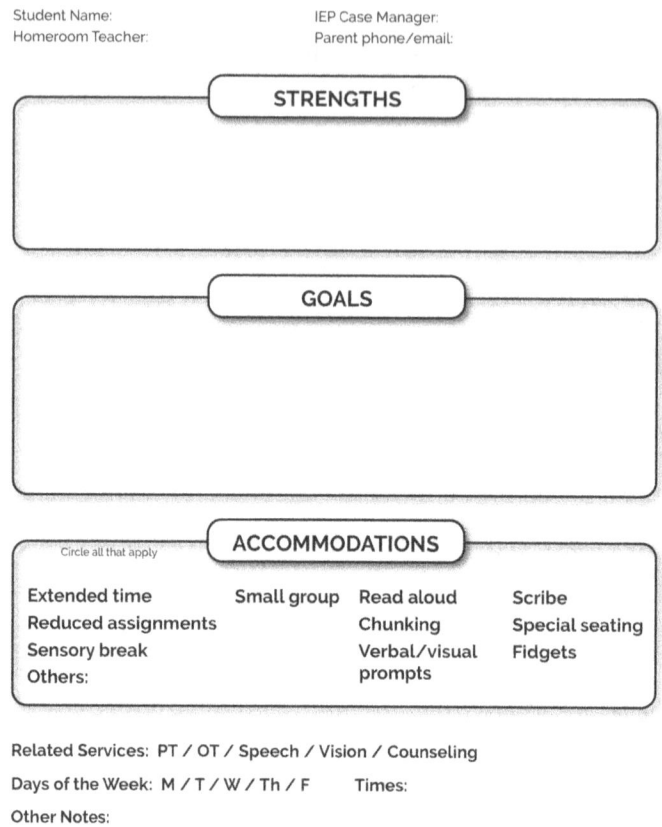

Figure 8.1 IEP at a Glance

Although I have seen these written in various ways, I list strengths at the top as I want that to be the primary focus. I include abbreviated goals and the accommodations the student needs in the classroom setting.

I created another one-page document for middle school and high school teachers. As they often have multiple students coming in and out of their classroom daily, this document helps them know who receives accommodations (Figure 8.2).

Co-Planning

Co-planning is an essential cornerstone in building a support team around a student. Unfortunately, many schools do not provide this time for their teachers as they do not see it as a priority. As an intensive needs teacher at a

Discovering Concerns and Fears 55

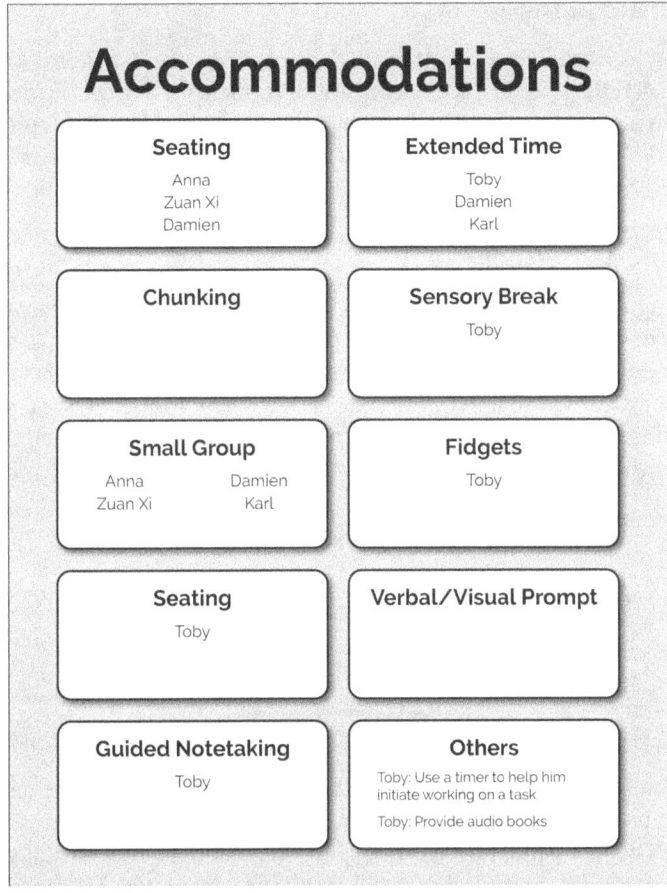

Figure 8.2 Example of Class-Wide Student Accommodations at a Glance

past school, the administration allotted me 20–30 minutes a month to meet with the general education teachers. 20–30 minutes! As you can imagine, this was not an adequate amount of time and only created resentment between the teachers and me as neither party felt supported. I thought the teachers didn't work hard enough for the students on my caseload and they thought I didn't teach them HOW to work with these students. It was a lose-lose situation. Therefore, co-planning time must be prioritized and built into the schedule.

At the very least, as learning support teachers, we need to build in frequent check-ins with general educators to ensure we are all on the same page. These check-ins help create trust and validation that we know their job is difficult. They need to know that we are always there to support them.

Practice Universal Design

According to Katie Novak, author of multiple books on Universal Design for Learning (UDL), "UDL is an education framework based on decades of research in neuroscience and endorsed by Every Student Succeeds Act. UDL is considered best practice for teaching all students in an inclusive learning environment (2021)."

All Students. ALL Students

As learning support teachers, it is our role to help general educators understand the concept of UDL. When we plan for our highest needs learners, all students benefit. We give students a voice and choice. We allow them to show us what they learned in a manner that plays to their strengths. We ensure that our learning goals do NOT inadvertently assess an area in which a student struggles, which creates a barrier.

> *When we plan for our highest needs learners, all students benefit.*

Salvador had a specific learning disability in writing. His teacher gave all the students a test and they had to write two paragraphs explaining the water cycle in detail. The assessment aimed to ensure the students understood the water cycle and explain it. Salvador knew all about the water cycle. He proved that by talking about it at length with his parents and me. But he failed the test.

Why? The assessment tested his writing ability rather than the actual content. I persuaded the teacher to let Salvador record himself talking about the water cycle. Ultimately, he showed his learning on the topic and passed the test. This simple change allowed him to use his strength rather than his weakness.

Here is an infographic from Dr. Novak which best explains UDL (reprinted with permission) (Figure 8.3).

Gain Perspective

It's funny. Whenever I enter a new work situation, I tell myself, "Always assume positive intentions." That's all well and good until I encounter a teacher who complains about students. My instinct is to get defensive and combative. However, that does no one any good. Instead, I listen. I listen to their venting. I peel back the layers and gain their perspective. I often understand where they are coming from and, more importantly, how I can better support them. It's truly as simple as that. Gain perspective and help support. When teachers feel heard

Discovering Concerns and Fears 57

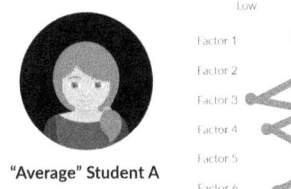

Figure 8.3 Universal Design for Learning UDL

and understood, they are more likely to become more inclusive. They know there is someone there who helps guide them along the way. They know you are in their corner.

When we have trust, we lay the groundwork for building Collective Efficacy.

In conclusion, confronting the concerns and fears of general education teachers when it comes to including students with special needs is a critical step toward building a more inclusive, accommodating, and nurturing learning environment. From the common refrain of "I'm not trained for this", it's clear that many teachers fear the unknown, their own inadequacy, and failure to meet their students' needs. Yet, the problem lies not in these educators' commitment or will but often in the lack of sufficient, relevant training and support. To tackle this issue, we must prioritize inclusion, strengthen teacher preparation programs, and foster a collective, schoolwide belief in the potential and rights of every student. It's not about creating a perfect system overnight; instead, it's about cultivating empathy, promoting understanding, and taking baby steps toward progress. Together, we can help our teachers see beyond the "disability", acknowledge the unique strengths within each student, and make our classrooms the enriching, welcoming spaces they are meant to be.

Reflection Questions

1 **Empathy and Understanding**: Reflecting on the story of Zeke and his general education teacher, how do personal biases and misconceptions about disabilities impact the educational experience of students with special needs? How can educators challenge these biases in themselves and their colleagues?
2 **Inadequate Preparation**: The chapter highlights a significant gap in the training general education teachers receive regarding special education and inclusion. Why is it essential for all educators, regardless of their specialization, to be equipped with the tools and understanding to support diverse learners? How can school districts and higher education institutions address this training gap?
3 **Universal Design for Learning (UDL)**: How does the concept of UDL challenge traditional methods of teaching and assessment? Reflect on Salvador's story about the water cycle test. How can educators ensure that their assessments truly measure a student's understanding of content rather than inadvertently testing unrelated skills?
4 **Building Collective Efficacy**: The chapter emphasizes the importance of collaboration, co-planning, and building Collective Efficacy among educators. Why is it crucial for learning support teachers and general educators to work closely together? How can schools create a culture where all educators feel empowered and supported to teach every student, regardless of their individual needs?

9 Discovering the Realities of a Diagnosis
It's Hard

Written by Lori

The next chapter is written from the viewpoint of a parent raising a child with special needs, specifically autism and intellectual delay. It's a deeply personal and emotional account that details the unique challenges, frustrations, grief, and ultimately, acceptance and advocacy that come with this experience. It is written for other parents facing similar challenges, educators, therapists, and anyone else who may interact with or want to understand the experience of families navigating the complexities of raising a child with special needs. The aim of the chapter is to foster empathy and compassion toward these families and to shed light on their often-underrepresented experiences and emotions.

Parenting is hard. It is, of course, a rewarding and wonderful role many of us jump into with great expectations and high hopes that our children will grow into happy, well-adjusted adults who experience some level of success. The definition of success is different for everyone. For some families, success means their child is admitted into an Ivy League school or becomes a doctor, lawyer, or Hollywood director. For others, success might mean their child grows up and has a family of their own. For some, success is when their child develops a particular skill or talent and can live their life being passionate about what they do. For most, the one definition of success is that their child is healthy and happy. This journey, or path, toward a child's success is often complicated and full of false starts, detours, and frustrations.

Now let's think about a family with a child who has special needs. Not only does the path get substantially more difficult, with potholes, speed bumps, and dead ends, but their definition of success must change as well.

When our son was young and we realized he had some differences in his development, we took a step back and reassessed his path. We understood that he would need special education. We understood his schooling would be different from his sister's. We thought, "Well, he is developmentally *delayed*, so he will learn these skills. It will just take him longer to learn them." It never occurred to us that our son would never talk. That he would never learn to read or write. That he would never learn to count to 20. That he would never become fully potty-trained.

DOI: 10.4324/9781032634357-11

So yes, the definition of success had to change and was frequently adjusted as he grew older. Imagine the sadness when in his IEP meetings year after year, we were told he didn't meet his goals. Imagine seeing the same goals on his IEP when he was sixteen as when he was six. "No, we don't care at this age if Braden learns his colors or his ABCs, which you've been trying to teach him for the past ten years. Can we try to teach him something that would be more beneficial for his life?"

Grief. It's real. I realize that admitting this is fodder for angry responses. As a society, we are inundated with videos and news stories shining a positive light on the experiences of people with disabilities (e.g., ASD): Greta Thunberg, who describes her autism as her "superpower" and has been nominated for a Nobel Peace Prize on more than one occasion. A teenager with Down syndrome is nominated for prom queen. The viral video of a high school basketball manager who gets put in to play the final few minutes of a game and proceeds to score a record-breaking number of three-point shots. The video of a man taken into a helicopter who can then recreate a perfect sketch of the skyline after only having seen it for a few moments.

Don't get me wrong, these are all fantastic accomplishments; however, these accolades and achievements set many families up to feel like they must always view their child's disability positively. Trying to view everything related to our child's disability in a positive light can create a sense of toxic positivity wherein families feel they can never admit they are struggling or grieving. They can never admit that IT'S HARD.

Side story "No, He's Not a Piano Prodigy." (Blog post written September 2016, updated August 2023)

Braden is autistic. Not only is he autistic, but he has an intellectual developmental delay. What does this mean for him? It means that he is almost always locked inside his own world. He can communicate with us to tell us what he wants or needs. If he doesn't know the word for it, he says "Yeah" to signify he wants something. Mike and I guess until we get it right.

- He can roller skate, snow ski, and climb jungle gyms.
- He cannot read, write, or draw a picture.
- He can follow one-step directions.
- He cannot follow multi-step directions.
- He can work the iPad to bring up YouTube videos.

He has very poor fine motor skills, so holding a pencil or a paintbrush is very difficult.

He is not a piano prodigy. He cannot tell us the number of toothpicks that have fallen on the ground without counting them. He is not able to tell you the day of the week that a certain date falls on. In other words, he is not a savant.

Many people believe that children with autism, especially nonverbal children with autism, have a special skill. I've had many people innocently ask me what Braden's special talent is. I always feel like I'm letting them down when I say he doesn't have one.

"He has phenomenal balance, though!" I always say. And it's true. He does have outstanding balance. One day I looked out the window of our Colorado home. He climbed up to our neighbor's jungle gym, was walking on top of the monkey bars ... and wearing roller skates! Unfortunately, this skill also got him in trouble quite a bit. More than one school playground official told us that Braden could not be at the top of the play equipment as although it wasn't hurting him, it gave all the other kids the idea they could do it too. Sigh ... try dragging your child with autism and IDD down from a jungle gym only to try to explain that he can't do his favorite thing. Yeah, that's fun.

Is a great sense of balance savant-like? No, but it's all I have to give. And since I'm proud of that in him, I share it willingly with people who ask me this question.

But not all kids with autism have a special skill like we've seen in movies such as *Rain Man*. Every time I read or see a story of an autistic prodigy, I smile. I celebrate for the families. I also cry inside a little and think, "What could I have done differently? How could I have helped develop this special talent for Braden?" But this is the reality of the situation. As Dr. Stephen Shore says, "If you've met one person with autism, you've met ONE person with autism" (Flannery and Wisner-Carlson, 2020). Each brain is different, and these kids with these amazing skills have something lighting up in their brains that Braden hasn't developed.

So, for now, I treasure those times I see Braden climbing and using those fantastic balancing skills of his. Who knows? Maybe one day, I'll knock a box of toothpicks onto the floor and Braden will say, "324 toothpicks." I doubt that will ever happen, considering we've never actually bought toothpicks.

Let's get back to grief and I want to make this very clear. I do not grieve because my child is disabled. My husband and I love both of our children and they make us proud on a daily basis. But I do grieve, and here are some reasons why.

My son has digestion problems that cause him to be in extreme pain. He cannot express that he's in pain in any other way but by breaking something or showing aggression. Or he will lay in bed completely despondent. A 2014 analysis based on almost 300,000 children in the United States revealed that children with autism are 67% more likely than typical children to have a diagnosis of irritable bowel syndrome (IBS). Numerous studies indicate gastrointestinal (GI) problems are pervasive among people with autism. The study suggests that children with autism are about four times as likely as other children to have symptoms such as constipation, diarrhea, or abdominal discomfort (McElhanon et al., 2014). I grieve because he is in pain, and I cannot help him feel better despite specialized diets, which took hours of time to research, plan, and implement, and despite multiple trips to the doctor for x-rays and blood tests. Despite everything we tried, he remains in pain. I grieve for him as he has never lived a pain-free existence. Pain free? That, to me, would be living a successful life.

I grieve because he has never had a friend. Braden is nonverbal and does not have an effective method of communication that others understand. He has never made a friend. I grieved every single time there was a birthday party in the past 22 years of his life and he didn't get an invitation. I grieve when I go to Starbucks and see a group of friends chatting, laughing, and being silly. Braden has never been part of a "group of friends." I know how much I love and value my friendships and I grieve the fact that he has none. It pains me to think of him recognizing this and how he must feel because of it.

I grieved for Braden when my friends' children attended their proms, played on sports teams, or graduated middle school, high school, and college. I lamented the fact that he never got to experience these milestone events. How many soccer games, basketball games, music concerts, and graduations did he watch of his sisters? Was he ever thinking, "Why can't I participate in those too?" I grieve the fact that I couldn't make that happen for him.

I grieve that Braden will not ever be part of a romantic relationship, never experience a schoolyard crush, never have his heart broken, never get married (if that's what he wanted) or have kids of his own. He will never experience a first kiss. And darn it, that makes me sad.

So, I don't grieve because he is disabled. I grieve because the effects of his particular autism and intellectual delay have created a life of pain for him, both physically and emotionally. No one wants that for their child.

> *I don't grieve because he has special needs. I grieve because the effects of his particular autism and intellectual delay have created a life of pain for him, both physically and emotionally.*

The stages of grief are well known (Kübler-Ross, 1969). They are:

1 Shock and Denial
2 Anger
3 Depression and Desolation
4 Dialogue and Bargaining
5 Acceptance
6 Return to Meaningful Life

When we think of grief, we tend to think about death. However, people can and do experience grief in many areas, including loss of a pet, moving, a change in health, loss of financial security, and more. We know that grief may come in waves and, through time, may eventually become easier once you've reached the acceptance stage and can return to a meaningful life stage. We also know that triggers may bring the grieving individual back through time, such as birthdays and holidays.

Grief in parenting a special needs child has a similar trajectory but is more of a roller coaster of sorts with its dips, long climbs, and the freefall that happens when you least expect it. Or, if you think in terms of the Snakes and Ladders game, it's like when you make it to the end of the gameboard, only to roll a one and end up back at the very beginning of the game.

To explain, I'll use my family's journey.

Shock and Denial

When Braden was first showing signs that he was not developing in a typical fashion, we were in a bit of denial.

"Well, his sister is doing all the speaking for him."

"He's hearing two languages. Maybe he just can't figure out which one to use."

"Well, I hear some kids don't learn to speak until later and they are just fine."

After finally deciding that his development was, in fact, atypical, we attempted to seek a diagnosis.

Anger

Did we go through the anger stage when Braden received his diagnosis? No, not before or upon diagnosis. If anything, we were relieved to have a word to name what was happening with him. The anger came later. The anger came when strangers gave us dirty looks or chastised us for our son's behavior. The anger came when asked to leave the bowling alley, the water park, the children's library, and various restaurants due to our child's loud voice. The anger happened when Braden's inability to communicate his needs effectively caused him to have a meltdown and injure himself. And this anger we experienced happened *throughout* Braden's childhood and even now as an adult. We experience anger, not due to the diagnosis, not due to autism, but at how Braden is treated as a member of society. We grieve that society is not as inclusive as it should be and it is anger inducing. We are angry that we, as his parents, could not figure out an efficient way for him to communicate, leaving him voiceless.

Depression and Detachment

Although our son is now an adult, whenever those triggers happen, the ones that cause us to feel upset and angry, we inevitably fall into a depression which we (my husband and I) experience differently. Mine manifests in stomach aches and a need to sleep, while my husband feels the need to "take control" of the situation and can't rest until everything is going in the direction he wants.

It is estimated that insomnia affects 50–80% of individuals with autism (Sarris, 2017). It certainly affected Braden and, in turn, affected us, his family. Mike and I "took turns" on who stayed up with Braden all night long and who got to sleep. Ultimately, we both were incredibly sleep deprived, which impacted our moods significantly. We had brain fog, low energy, compromised immune systems, and I went into a deep depression. I woke up each morning wanting to cry for seemingly no reason. Of course, there was a reason. I was exhausted and stressed. But my brain kept telling me nothing was wrong. I sought medical intervention for my depression, and I'm thankful I did. While my sleep didn't improve, my outlook on life did, and I could function better as a mother and family member.

At age 21, our son moved to a residential program to live. He still does not sleep. And sadly, neither do we. Years of sleeping with "one eye open" have manipulated our brains to think we need to wake up several times per night. While certainly not ideal, we are used to it and have figured out how to function on little sleep. This is not recommended as sleep is necessary to maintain good health, but for us, it is what it is.

The depression now hits us when we least expect it. Braden will be going along just fine and happy when he has a setback suddenly. We have gotten the dreaded phone call, "Braden broke the toilet in the house and then broke everything that he called 'brown,' so basically, yeah, he broke all the wooden furniture."

There we are at the top of the roller coaster, that moment when our stomachs drop away from us, and we are freefalling. Bam! Back down to the depression stage of grief. And so, it goes … up and down … up and down.

Dialogue and Bargaining

I undertook and earned my master's degree in special education in the dialogue and bargaining stage. I needed to talk about Braden's autism often. I needed to find others to discuss my newfound knowledge and understanding of autism and I had to start making sense of it all. At this time, my husband started an autism podcast so we could learn from experts in the field.

Acceptance

Accepting the diagnosis, for us, was not hard. We had met other autistic individuals who had gone on to lead wonderful lives, live independently, and work in a field they are passionate about; all those indicators of success mentioned earlier. We were encouraged by these stories. So, we accepted his diagnosis, knowing his road would be more difficult but also having hope for his healthy and happy life ahead.

Accepting our son's place in society is much more difficult. So, although we came to the point of acceptance of his diagnosis with little to no trouble, the constant and daily reminders that society does not accept our son starts the whole grief cycle again.

Like the time we were at Disneyland. We were in an extremely crowded space and Braden's sensory system was overwhelmed and he became dysregulated. I got down next to him and tried to calm him down with a quiet voice and soothing tone. Suddenly a woman turned around, bent down to Braden's face, and shushed him. I tried explaining to the woman that he had autism and his sensory system was unhappy, but she didn't care. She said he was ruining her experience and that wasn't fair.

So yeah, we went to Disneyland, and what do I remember from that trip? That story, because that experience served as a reminder that society needs to do better. Cue the loud screaming as my roller coaster car just plummeted again and we are back to depression.

Return to Meaningful Life

I will never grieve the fact that my son has special needs. Because of him, I became a special education teacher. I found my true passion, advocating for inclusion. Many parents of special needs children find themselves in similar advocate-type roles. For some, their children help provide meaning.

There are many reasons I'm thankful for my son's diagnosis. I joined a community I never knew I would be a part of, and special needs families are some of the coolest people I've ever met. I'm thankful that my son needs to constantly move as he has kept us motivated to stay in shape and healthy to support him better. I'm grateful to have the inclusion lens on everything I encounter and advocate for change if need be.

But I grieve. Yes. I grieve. And other families grieve too. And their grief comes and goes. Grief can be triggered by something small. It can be triggered by something large. It can be triggered by an actual or perceived slight or threat. And if we're triggered, we plummet down the rails again.

My hope by sharing this story with you is not to gain sympathy. No, none of us need that. However, a fair bit of empathy can go a very long way.

All parents agree that we want our children to be healthy and happy as a marker of success. Some of us who have children with profound exceptional needs have little certainty that what we do will ensure a healthy and happy human. Therefore, we grieve.

What do families need from their community?

Compassion. Compassion from teachers, therapists, and fellow community members is imperative to support families during the extraordinary lows and highs of the roller coaster ride of their life.

Navigating the roller coaster of emotions that comes with parenting a special needs child is an experience that words can often barely capture. As I shared the story of my family's journey with Braden, it's clear that grief isn't a singular event; it's a continuous process, an ebb and flow tied intrinsically to our love and hopes for our child. Raising Braden has been a lesson in resilience, in understanding the depths of human emotion, and in confronting the societal norms and challenges head-on. What I hope others can glean from our story isn't pity or sorrow, but a profound appreciation for the power of empathy. It's through understanding each other that we truly build bridges of connection. Every parent's wish is for their child to lead a meaningful life filled with health and happiness. While our journey might have more dips and turns than most, it's a journey made richer through shared understanding and compassion from others.

Reflection Questions

1 **Understanding Grief**: How can educators apply the understanding of the stages of grief, as described in the context of parenting a special needs child, to better support students and their families?
2 **Promoting Inclusivity in Educational Settings**: The chapter underscores societal challenges and perceptions of individuals with special needs through the experiences of Braden and his family. As an educator, have you witnessed similar reactions or behaviors in the school setting? How can educational environments be adjusted to encourage more inclusivity and understanding?
3 **Empathy vs. Sympathy**: Lori shares her thoughts on empathy vs. sympathy. Reflect on your interactions with students and their families. How do you ensure that your approach leans more toward empathy, and what strategies can you implement to promote empathetic behaviors among students?
4 **Supporting Emotional Well-being in Special Needs Education**: Given the roller coaster metaphor used to depict the emotional journey of families with special needs, how can educators be better equipped to support not just the academic but also the emotional well-being of these students? How might you adapt your teaching strategies to account for the potential "highs and lows" these students and their families may experience?

Discovering the Realities of a Diagnosis 67

In the Discovering section, we hope you got a glimpse into the different perspectives of parents, teachers, and therapists as they discover they are working with or have a child with a disability.

We took you through the process of the initial understanding of the diagnostic process and the complex nature of what it entails. We gave you information about what goes into this stage of the process and a sample of how parents may respond to this newfound diagnosis.

We uncovered how this process affects one another differently. The overwhelmingness, the groundlessness, the anxiety about their child's future, and the grief felt by parents. The confusion and frustration felt by teachers before unearthing that their student has a special need. We introduced the process and interpretation of a comprehensive evaluation. Arming ourselves with information establishes a common understanding, which helps alleviate confusion surrounding what is going on with our child or student. Alleviating this confusion then sets the stage for clarity and compassion in supporting one another.

Now we move into the next section, Navigating. Once members of the collaborative team discover an individual with whom they interact has a disability, what happens next to help build the Collective Efficacy of that team?

This section shares more of our stories and strategies gained from our experiences. We share Lori's point of view as a parent and teacher and Amanda's as a psychologist in order to continue our journey of what happens next. We highlight some wisdom we acquired along the way. We posit some new ideas to continue this evolution of building Collective Efficacy.

We now know that we can accomplish this through improved communication, understanding, and compassion, and advocating in the child's best interest.

Part II
Navigating

10 Navigating Through the Educational Jargon

Enough With the Acronyms Already

Written by Lori

This next chapter is written from a parent perspective, addressing the complexities of educational jargon, especially as it pertains to special needs. It emphasizes the educator's role in ensuring clarity and support for parents who might be overwhelmed by the myriad of terms and acronyms. The chapter is written for both educators and parents, urging educators to be more transparent and patient while empowering parents to seek clarity and understanding in their child's educational journey. The chapter underscores the importance of collaboration between parents and educators.

I was an elementary school teacher for ten years before my son Braden received his diagnosis. I had heard my share of acronyms in the educational context. But once I had a child with special needs, acronym usage hit a whole new level.

In a slightly exaggerated format, this is what my husband and I heard at some of our first meetings.

> Mr. and Mrs. Boll, we gave Braden a series of assessments, including the PPVT, WISC, ADOS, and ABLES. His PPVT and WISC showed an extremely low IQ score with a SS of 45. As we read through the ADOS, it appears Braden does have ASD, which would take away his diagnosis of PPD-NOS. He may also have APD and an ID.
>
> As you know, under IDEA and the ADA, Braden is entitled to a FAPE. The SST has scheduled Braden's first IEP meeting. We will go over his goals and objectives with the multi-disciplinary SPED team, which includes the teacher, OT, SLP, and educational psychologist. At this meeting, we will discuss whether we will use ABA, VBA, a combination of both, or the SCERTS model with Braden based on his needs.

As hyperbolic as this passage is, parents can genuinely feel like they are in a version of Charlie Brown and a *Peanuts* cartoon when his teachers or parents are talking. There are a lot of words, but nothing truly makes sense.

We know you are not using all these acronyms at once when meeting with families. But it can feel this way for families who are recently comprehending a diagnosis and learning what this means for their child.

As educators and professionals, we have been doing this for a while. We know the ins and outs of assessment, what the scores mean, how to interpret the scores, and how to plan an Individualized Education Plan based on those scores and your daily interactions with the student. Parents? They are entirely new to this. Think of it this way: adults are given their driver's license and learn how to operate their basic automobile. Then they have their child, and suddenly this car's operating instructions just got a lot more complicated. Soon, they get a diagnosis for their child and they are suddenly trying to operate the Millennium Falcon. There are so many buttons and gadgets. These parents are petrified that one wrong move will send them into hyperspace and they will have no way of knowing if they went in the right direction or not.

So as educators and professionals, our duty is to be forthcoming, transparent, and supportive.

> *... As educators and professionals, our duty is to be forthcoming, clear, and supportive.*

Be Forthcoming

When sharing a diagnosis or meeting with families, we must be truthful and transparent. We need to explicitly state the diagnosis (and not use an acronym). We need to tell them what this diagnosis means, both medically and educationally. We need to share the next steps in terms of treatment therapies and how this will look in school.

Be Clear

I worked with a family in Shanghai, China, who received a report from a psychologist about their 14-year-old son who was not performing well in his international school. It was a clear report for me, a special educator, as I had read many before and knew how to interpret them. But this family was clearly confused. The child's IQ stated a Standard Score of 75. His parents based their understanding of this score on a 100-point scale, so they assumed that 75 meant their child was dead average. Honestly, it's a fair assumption, right?

So, I had to draw the bell curve for them and show them that 100 actually meant average and then show them where a 75 fell. I can't ever forget that moment. The parents' faces fell. It wasn't until they saw this in a visual format that they understood the interpretation of the score. And here I was, a teacher, having to be the one who shared this news with them.

Was it the psychologist's fault, or did these parents simply misunderstand what the psychologist was trying to tell them? Either way, it was apparent that it wasn't clear what these assessment results meant and how they should proceed.

This ambiguity is just one example of which I have many from my career as a special educator. It has always made me wonder how we can do better.

So, we must be clear.

Provide a timeline or structure of expectations. Provide a list of commonly used acronyms. We don't want to overwhelm our families, so only give them the acronyms that will apply to their child.

Be Supportive

Will parents take this all in the first time? No, probably not. Parents are on a journey of learning and understanding their child's needs. And remember that they are trying to operate the Millennium Falcon with very little information to go on.

It takes time to learn how to operate this complicated vehicle. Han Solo did not learn it overnight. He spent countless hours learning and practicing. He also had teachers and co-pilots to support him.

We must be our parents' co-pilots and help them through this complicated process. And we need to give them time and patience as they learn. The more we can partner with our families in this process, the more trust we develop with each other. With trust comes more understanding and progress in reaching all our goals when working with their children.

Han Solo could not have done it without Chewbacca. And our parents can't navigate this journey without our support.

The more we can partner with our families in this process, the more trust we develop with each other. With trust comes more understanding and progress in reaching all our goals when working with their children.

In the unchartered waters of acronyms, complex assessments, and endless educational jargon, we have a crucial role to play. We must remember to be forthcoming, clear, and supportive. We should aim to demystify the diagnosis, explain its implications, and lay out a roadmap for parents to navigate through this new terrain. Strive for clarity in your communication and give a comprehensive, yet concise, overview of the relevant acronyms that parents need to know. Support is not a one-time act but a commitment to stand by our parents as they grapple with the nuances of this challenging journey. Remember, you are the co-pilot to these parents in their Millennium Falcon. It is through our trustful and supportive partnership that we can achieve our shared goals and ensure every child's needs are met. Just as Han Solo needed Chewbacca, our parents need us. In this seemingly endless sea of acronyms and jargon, let us be their beacon of clarity and guide them toward understanding and growth.

Reflection Questions

1. **Bridging the Gap Between Educators and Parents**: After reading Lori's experiences and the analogy of parents trying to operate the Millennium Falcon, how do you perceive your current communication style with parents? Are there any areas where you think you can simplify or clarify your language to avoid overwhelming them with jargon?
2. **The Importance of Visual Tools**: Lori provided an example of drawing the bell curve for a family to help them understand their child's IQ score. How often do you utilize visual aids or tools when explaining complex concepts or results to parents? Can you think of a situation where a visual tool might have made a significant difference in a parent's understanding?
3. **Continuous Support and Trust Building**: Reflecting on Lori's emphasis on being supportive and the importance of trust, what strategies or practices do you currently implement to foster trust with parents, especially those new to navigating special education? Are there any new methods you might consider after reading this chapter?
4. **Assessment Clarity and Interpretation**: The example with the family from Shanghai highlighted potential misconceptions parents might have when interpreting assessment results. Based on your experience, what are common misconceptions parents have regarding their child's assessment results? How can you better prepare to address these misunderstandings proactively?

11 Navigating Concerns Relating to Educational Setting

School Placement and Goodness of Fit

Written by Dr. Ly

The next chapter is written by a school psychologist and is intended for teachers, administrators, educational professionals, and parents involved with or interested in the education of children with special needs. The content focuses on inclusion and the ascertaining of the proper educational environment, offering insights and resources relevant to those working with students with disabilities.

> *Separate is inherently unequal. We understand this in terms of racial segregation, but not as it pertains to educating those with special learning needs.*

Separate is inherently unequal. We understand this in terms of racial segregation, but not as it pertains to educating those with special learning needs.

"Separate Educational Facilities are inherently unequal" (Earl Warren, Supreme Court Justice delivering the ruling on *Brown v. Board of Education* in 1954.)

School Placement. Goodness of Fit

Schools matter. Teachers matter more. While school placement is of the utmost importance in determining whether or not a child will succeed, the child's teacher actually matters even more. In fact, as part of a large, longitudinal study (ongoing and spanning several years) during graduate school, we followed ALL the teachers and ALL the students in the entire state, showing just that. The findings were clear that teachers matter. For the people in the back, "GOOD TEACHERS MATTER THE MOST!" To explain that in a very clear way – no matter what risk factors a student exhibited, good teachers could be effective with them. The research accounted for all sorts of variables, including prior achievement, gender, race, a marker for low income (e.g., free/reduced lunch status), gifted, emotionally disturbed, specific learning disability, mild mental retardation (aka mild intellectual disability), special education status, student attendance, how often a student has moved, and disciplinary variables (i.e., suspension expulsion, etc.). Throughout our research, year after year, the good teachers were consistently effective with students and "bad teachers" were consistently somewhat effective or even ineffective with students.

Schools Matter. Teachers Matter MORE!

Note – "Bad" teachers are not necessarily a reflection of personality or personal characteristics but are more a reflection of "bad" or inadequate training programs. The data looked back at the teacher training programs and the long-term effectiveness throughout a teacher's career. On the flip side, a "good" teacher is the product of a "good" teacher training program.

Mainstreaming and Inclusion

The Individuals with Disabilities Education Act of 1997b (IDEA 97) requires that students are in the "least restrictive environments" (LRE). The least restrictive environment is typically the general education classroom because this is where the student is placed if they do not have a disability.

There are two key ways of including students in the LRE: mainstreaming and inclusion. Mainstreaming and inclusion are often used interchangeably, but they are two different systems.

Mainstreaming refers to keeping disabled students in the regular education classroom for specific classes and then separating them for others (Rogers, 1993). Generally, under this system, the student must be able to keep up with the work assigned to them with reasonable support/assistance to stay in the classroom. Mainstreaming came about after an article written in 1968 in which the author, Dunn, pointed out problems with separating disabled students from the general education classroom. This article also laid the groundwork for key components of the Education for All Handicapped Children Act, which later became the Individuals with Disabilities Education Act.

Inclusion refers to allowing the student to remain in the regular education classroom as much as possible. The supports are then brought to that child. In the U.S., there has been a significant push for inclusion. Students not segregated from their nondisabled peers is the central tenet. Many classrooms intend to be inclusive but then simply end up replicating special education services in the general education classroom. In these contexts, disabled students are commonly segregated within general education. "The ultimate goal of inclusion is to make an increasingly wider range of differences ordinary in a general education classroom" (McLeskey & Waldron, 2007, p. 163).

McLeskey and Waldron (2007) discuss ways to achieve inclusion. First, create a classroom where varying behaviors are more tolerated/accepted and thus become a routine part of the regular education classroom while utilizing supports. This tolerance will aid the school community in learning to accept a larger variety of differences and become more commonplace in school (McLeskey & Waldron, 2007). Within a typical general education classroom, students display a broad range of academic and social skills. Teachers naturally or automatically arrange their classrooms to accommodate these different ranges of student abilities/levels. Some students do not fall within this acceptable range and may require special services. For inclusion to be successful, teachers need to expand their "level of tolerance" so these students can remain in the mainstream classroom. McLeskey and Waldron (2007) encourage inclusion educators to maintain the "rhythm of a typical classroom." They mean that the schedule, curriculum, and entire school day of a special needs student should be as similar as possible to general education students. The big idea from McLeskey and Waldron's (2007) work is that all students must become part of the learning and social community of the classroom. Students with disabilities must therefore be considered "regular" and included in the general education classroom just the same as those without disabilities. This final big idea will require that many teachers challenge their assumptions about disabled students.

There is a long list of benefits for ALL STUDENTS explaining why we should strive for inclusivity (not just in school but in many arenas ... that is for another book). A short list of benefits from Begeny and Martens (2007) includes:

- Improvement in academics
- Increased social skills
- More apt to live in the community with little assistance
- Improving teacher skills
- Helping students develop more positive attitudes toward others with disabilities
- Establishing
- social principles based on equality

Historically, the special education system in the United States has been shown to be not that effective. As per the 14th Annual Report to Congress (U.S. Department of Education, 1992):

- 57% of special education students graduate with a diploma or certificate of graduation
- Once identified, less than 5% of all students (including students with SLD) leave special education

The National Longitudinal Transition Study (NASBE, 1992) showed that:

- 49% of special education students aged 15–20 were employed two years after graduation
- 13.4% were living independently

The conclusion drawn by the NASBE 1992 Study Group on Special Education cited that these aforementioned results were mainly due to the "unnecessary segregation and labeling of children with disabilities. Additionally, the 'ineffective practice of mainstreaming' has had negative effects on students both academically and socially." (Brucker, 1994).

As mentioned earlier in the Discovering section, a multi-tiered system of support (MTSS) should be implemented across the entire student body to best support the early identification of students with learning and behavioral challenges. A MTSS helps identify students with special needs, implement the appropriate level/intensity of intervention, and monitor to ensure adequate progress.

As a recap, Tier 1, or universal/schoolwide support and instruction, is provided to all students and a majority of students (approximately 75–90%) respond well to this support. Tier 2 supports are more specialized interventions that meet the needs of the 5–15% of students who do not respond effectively to tier 1 supports. Tier 3 supports are more intensive, individualized interventions that typically meet the needs of the 3–5% of students who do not respond effectively to tier 1 or 2 supports.

The MTSS framework includes processes for screening all students, providing tiered instruction and intervention support, and monitoring students' progress. (Burns et al., 2016; Zumeta Edmonds, 2016). The multitiered framework addresses problems early for at-risk students for poor learning outcomes. Schools identify struggling learners through universal screening. They provide multiple tiers of evidence-based instruction and interventions, monitor student progress, and adjust the intensity and nature of those interventions depending on their responsiveness. When indicated, schools help identify students with learning disabilities or other disabilities according to state and district guidance (Center on Response to Intervention & National Center on Intensive Intervention, 2014).

MTSS provides a method of early identification AND intervention that can help struggling students catch up with their peers. A list of evidence-based interventions that are appropriate for each tier of intervention delivered through an MTSS model can be found at The Center for Multi-Tiered System of Supports by The American Institute of Research website: https://mtss4success.org/

An additional resource comes from the National Center on Response to Intervention, funded by the U.S. Department of Education's Office of Special Education Programs, the American Institutes for Research, and researchers from Vanderbilt University and the University of Kansas. The Center provides technical assistance to states and districts and builds the capacity of states to assist districts in implementing proven Response to Intervention frameworks. If you would like more information on the National Center on Response to Intervention, see http://www.rti4success.org

The following are recommended key tenets to MTSS interventions aggregated from The Center for Multi-Tiered System of Supports and The National Center for Response to Intervention based on the tiers of MTSS:

Tier 1:
- Effective High-Quality Curriculum – a research-based core curriculum
- Instructional practices that are culturally and linguistically responsive
- Universal screening to determine students' current level of performance
- Differentiated learning activities (e.g., mixed instructional grouping, use of learning centers, peer tutoring) to address individual needs
- Accommodations to ensure all students have access to the instructional program
- Problem solving to identify interventions, as needed, to address behavior problems that prevent students from demonstrating the academic skills they possess

Tier 2:
- Involves small-group instruction that relies on evidence-based interventions that specify the instructional procedures, duration (typically 10–15 weeks of 20- to 40-minute sessions), and instruction frequency (three or four times per week)
- Three distinguishing characteristics of the intervention:
- Evidence-based
- Relies entirely on adult-led small-group rather than whole-class instruction
- Involves a clearly articulated and validated intervention

Tier 3:
- Individualized to target each student's area(s) of need
- More intensive version of the intervention program (e.g., longer sessions, smaller group size, more frequent sessions)
- The teacher conducts frequent progress monitoring (i.e., at least weekly) with each student
- The teacher engages in problem-solving processes should the data indicate the student's rate of progress is unlikely to achieve the established learning goal
- The teacher modifies components of the intervention program and continues to employ frequent progress monitoring to evaluate which elements enhance the rate of student learning. By continually monitoring and modifying (as needed) each student's program, the teacher can design an effective, individualized instructional program

In conclusion, the idea of inclusion and mainstreaming within the educational system underscores the profound importance of equitable learning environments and the value of effective teachers in supporting all learners. The role of a good teacher is pivotal in the success of any student, regardless of their learning needs. At the heart of this success is the necessity for strong, comprehensive teacher training programs that equip educators with the skills to be effective with a wide range of learners. Furthermore, the implementation of an MTSS across all educational settings ensures early identification and appropriate support for students with learning and behavioral challenges. It is essential that every child feels part of the learning community, with the classroom being a space that accommodates a broad spectrum of academic and social skills. The ultimate goal is to cultivate an educational environment that celebrates diversity, fosters inclusion, and challenges prevailing assumptions about students with disabilities. To attain this, we must continue to advocate for systematic change that places students and effective teaching at the center of all educational decisions. Schools matter, but remember, teachers matter more.

Reflection Questions

1 **Teacher's Impact and Training**: Reflecting on the statement "GOOD TEACHERS MATTER THE MOST!" and the discussion about teacher training programs, how do you think current educational systems can be improved to better prepare teachers for inclusion and mainstreaming? What would you suggest as key components of a teacher training program geared toward inclusivity?
2 **MTSS and Early Intervention**: Based on the MTSS presented, how does early identification and intervention contribute to the success of students with learning and behavioral challenges? How can schools ensure that they are effectively implementing each tier of the MTSS, and what are the potential consequences of not doing so?
3 **Benefits of Inclusivity Beyond Education**: The chapter discusses the benefits of inclusivity not only in educational settings but also in other arenas. How do you think the principles of inclusivity in the classroom translate to broader societal contexts, such as workplaces and public spaces? How can the lessons learned in inclusive classrooms inform more inclusive practices in other areas of life?
4 **Redefining "Regular" in Education**: Reflecting on the idea that "students with disabilities must therefore be considered "regular" and included in the general education classroom," how can educational institutions work to challenge and redefine societal perceptions and biases surrounding what is deemed "regular" or "normal"?

12 Navigating School Transitions

Written by Lori

The chapter that follows is written from an advocacy and informative perspective, focusing on the unique challenges that families with children who have special learning needs face when transitioning to new schools, especially international ones. The content draws on personal stories to illustrate the real-world difficulties, emphasizing the need for inclusivity and proper support within the education system. It is intended for parents of children with special needs, educators, school administrators, and policymakers, encouraging them to recognize and address the barriers to quality education for students with learning differences. The chapter serves both as a call to action for schools to enhance their support systems and a resource to help families understand and navigate these challenges.

In the international school world, moving is part of the package. The amount of time spent at any one school solely depends on employment contracts. Embassy employees sign a 3–5-year contract, engineers anywhere from 2–5 years, while other careers can stay as long as they wish if their host country provides them with a work visa.

Moving overseas or to another school can be extremely daunting for families who have children with different learning needs. Stress during these moves is high, and each family member handles this stress differently. Transitions can be challenging for each family member, whether they have special needs or not.

Parents often find themselves in a situation they never envisioned. International schools are not required to accept all children, so parents moving from a country where education is free and appropriate by law are suddenly moving to a country where these rules don't apply.

The typical trajectory of the process is as follows:

- One or both parents take a job in another country with multiple international schools
- Parents go online and search for international schools in their future home
- They then navigate the websites and type in "special education." At this point, parents discover that a) the school has no special education program; b) the school offers support for learners with students who have "mild"

needs; c) the school is inclusive, but the price of a program for their child with more intensive needs is extremely cost-prohibitive (often double the regular tuition)

These obstacles leave parents wondering what they should do. And often, they feel they only have two options:

- Give the school the information they ask for, answer all questions honestly, and know there is a very good chance their child will still be denied admission
- Be less forthcoming with the application

This decision probably seems evident to people who do not find themselves in this situation. Of course, they should tell the truth. But if we look at this from the family's perspective, this decision is anything but simple.

To illustrate, I'd like to share the story of Elizabeth and her family. Elizabeth's mom, Catherine, and her husband, Dave, moved to Shanghai, China, from the United Kingdom, for Dave's career when Elizabeth was in Grade 6.

> *We embarked on the journey, and it didn't really cross my mind that I would have difficulty getting my child into a school.*
> *—Catherine, Elizabeth's mother*

Elizabeth is on the autism spectrum. As this was in the early 2000s, her diagnosis at that time was Asperger's syndrome.

The first two schools Catherine investigated required an admissions test. Catherine decided they wouldn't be a good fit as, with her diagnosis, Elizabeth needed to know what the assessment looked like ahead of time to help with her anxiety around it, which the schools would not accommodate.

The third school looked promising. They invited the family in for an interview. It all went well until they began discussing Elizabeth's feet. Elizabeth was born with clubfoot. Clubfoot, also known as talipes equinovarus (TEV), is a common foot abnormality in which the foot points downward and inward (Nationwide Children's, 2004. The school asked if it would be difficult for Elizabeth to walk to her classes across the campus. Catherine assured them that Elizabeth would be fine and there were no concerns. At that point, Catherine asked about the school dress code policy. Part of the policy was that students must wear lace-up shoes. Due to the angle of Elizabeth's right foot, she couldn't wear lace-up shoes, so she needed to wear Crocs or sneakers. At that point, the school told them, "Well, if she doesn't meet our uniform requirements, she cannot attend our school." Catherine immediately jumped into protective mother mode and explained that they could buy shoes that looked laced. She honestly couldn't believe the school wouldn't make this simple accommodation. Finally, Dave looked at Catherine and said, "Listen, if it's going to be a fight over a simple pair of shoes, where are we going to go with all the other stuff?" After all, they hadn't even spoken about Elizabeth's academics yet. So, they walked away in search of another school.

The fourth school did not even consider Elizabeth's application. Naming themselves the pre-eminent international school in Shanghai, this school only catered to average to above-average students.

Finally, the family had success with the fifth school – or so they thought. Elizabeth was accepted, so Catherine and Dave also signed up their son and the two started school together. Within the first two weeks, the school identified that Elizabeth's math skills were below average. They had her go in after school to do more math practice. However, this intervention did not have its intended consequence and after four months, the school decided that she could no longer attend.

Sadly, the school did not consider that Elizabeth had top marks in English and Spanish classes. Because the school tied math with science, Elizabeth was failing two classes. With some negotiation on the parents' part, the school agreed to allow Elizabeth to stay under the condition that she receive outside tutoring and support.

And then, in Catherine's words, "the worst thing happened." The school hosted an awards ceremony for the students and their families. They called up students to the front at the ceremony who maintained a particular grade point average. In the end, every student in her class went up to receive a certificate, while Elizabeth was left sitting alone in her row.

At that point, Catherine looked at her husband and said, "We're out of here. I'm not fighting this anymore. Anybody who can be that cruel to leave one kid, with Asperger's, who can't really communicate, in a row, all by herself."

By then, Catherine was sobbing in the back of the room. "That was the last time Elizabeth set foot in that school."

What next? Homeschool. After several months of attempting this, it became clear that this was not a good option for the family.

So, they found yet another school and received a denial yet again.

They found another school and Elizabeth was accepted. This, may I remind you, is school number seven. She found much success there and she enjoyed it immensely. Sadly, some shady characters at that school ran away with all the money. The school shut down, leaving students without a school.

School number eight accepted Elizabeth. It was a brand-new school and she did well as she was one of the few English speakers in the school. Sadly, this school did not enter the students for the International General Certificate of Secondary Education (IGCSE) exams.

> The IGCSEs are a vital assessment in international schools that follow the British education system. Firstly, it is a benchmark to show that a student has a foundation to study further. Secondly, the IGCSEs symbolize achievement that shows that the student has the required knowledge to join the workplace (Perera, 2021).

The major consequence of not being entered into the exams was that there was ultimately no way Elizabeth would be successful back in the UK without taking them.

After eight schools, the family had had enough. They picked up and moved home to the UK to get Elizabeth the schooling she needed. "After all those years, Elizabeth left Shanghai with nothing," Catherine explained.

Since their return, Elizabeth passed her IGCSEs in all subject areas, including math!

> It wasn't as if she couldn't. It was because no school could see beyond the reports or the child who, because of her Asperger's, doesn't communicate well. Combined with the 'meh' report and a quiet child, schools just didn't want her. And then, once they did take her, they were looking for every reason to have her leave. They didn't want to have her take the IGCSEs as they were afraid she would bring the school exam results percentage down. And look, she passed them all.
>
> (Catherine)

In fact, she not only passed, she also earned high enough scores to get into university. The university accepted Elizabeth not on grade requirements but on her own merit. She interviewed on her own to get in. All her life, no one wanted her, but this university was excited to have her.

Elizabeth has one more year of university. Upon graduation, she will be qualified to be a special education teacher.

Eight schools. Eight schools failed Elizabeth. Eight schools let her and her family down. Eight schools did not see Elizabeth's gifts and only saw her disability. Eight schools.

Why do parents not tell the truth at times? Not everyone has had this level of rejection, but I've talked to many who have similar stories.

- Janet has a colostomy bag. The international school we applied to denied her immediately. I explained that I would come in each day at lunch to handle it, and it in no way impacts her academic abilities. But they were adamant in their stance. It was a hard no.
- They denied Michael because I checked the box saying he had an IEP at his previous school. He needed extra time on assessments. The school denied

him on this basis, as they "didn't make any testing accommodations." When I asked why, they just said, "It's our policy."
- I stupidly marked that Jason has ADHD. He was denied entry. The school told me they do not have the resources to support him. I never marked that box again. I learned my lesson.

Why do parents not always give all the information? They fear that they will end up in a similar situation as Elizabeth. They are fearful their child will be denied for ridiculous reasons.

Although many more international schools are becoming more inclusive, there are still many who are not, and this is simply unacceptable. Schools want parents to give them all the information and feel righteous in saying, "Well, it's better that we don't accept your child as we just don't have the resources to support them." How is this good for the families?

Table 12.1 is a chart we created after discussing the issue with admissions directors, heads of schools, principals of international schools throughout the world, and families themselves. The chart gives a clear overview of many reasons schools do not accept children with learning differences. On the other side of the chart are the parents' feelings and the sometimes-obvious questions about a school's thought process (or lack of one) surrounding inclusive practices.

Table 12.1 School and Family Point of View on School Placement

School Point of View	Family Point of View
We don't have the human resources to support all students and their learning needs.	In my child's last school, they just needed some pull-out time with the Learning Support teacher. Please let us explain how this worked rather than deny our application based on her diagnosis. OR Well, then you should *get* the resources to support these students.
We can't cater to the physical needs of some students (i.e., students in wheelchairs).	In our home country, this is mandated by law. OR You think that because my child has cerebral palsy, she cannot navigate the stairs, but you didn't ask us. That is an assumption you made, but it is incorrect. She is perfectly capable of getting around on her own. It takes her a bit longer, but she can do it. Please give us a chance to explain.
Our school is college preparatory, so we cannot cater to all learners.	My child will go to college. They need some support along the way. OR So, you are saying that you don't believe that every child has a right to learn?

(*Continued*)

Table 12.1 (Continued)

School Point of View	Family Point of View
Students with learning needs will bring down the overall test scores of our school.	The research proves otherwise. "While it is true that proficiency levels are low for students in special education, the bottom line is that for most schools, those scores have little impact on a school's overall proficiency level." (tcrain@al.com, 2017)
Parents should not move overseas if they have a child with learning needs.	Working overseas is our livelihood. We should not be penalized because our child has a learning difference. We must pay for our child's expensive therapies. We need this job.
Standards at our international school are very high and children with learning needs would not be able to access the curriculum.	My child attended school with their peers in my home country. Why wouldn't they be able to do the same here? OR They can access the curriculum with the correct accommodations in place. Give them the chance to show you they can.
Supporting students with additional learning needs is expensive, so we need to charge a high fee for your child to attend.	We already pay to have private therapy for our child. Now we must pay more in tuition so our children can go to school like their siblings? OR Have you thought about subsidizing education? Raise the tuition of all students so the few who need extra supports can get them without financially ruining the students who need them.
We wish parents would share the whole story.	We shared what we know about our child, how they worked at their old school, and how we see them at home. OR If we share that our child had support at their last school, you will deny them entry. But we know they will be okay. OR Please ask the right questions rather than screening our child out due to a diagnosis.

There are currently close to 9,500 international schools worldwide, and the number of international schools supporting students with special learning needs has increased significantly in the last ten years. According to a 2020 joint report done by ISC Research and Next Frontier Inclusion (NFI), 67% of the 207 international schools that participated have a learning support program. Make no mistake. Just because a school does not technically have students with learning disabilities on their registers does not mean they are not there. They're in the school and they need appropriate education. It's time for all schools to stop making false claims that they are unable to accept these students.

In the realm of international schools, the process of transition and adaptation for families with children with special needs can be a complex and taxing journey. The uncertainty of acceptance and the fear of rejection often provoke parents into making difficult decisions, including withholding information about their child's needs. The experiences shared by parents such as Catherine show us the unfortunate reality of numerous schools prioritizing uniform requirements or test scores over inclusive education, causing undue distress for families. Notably, the increasing presence of learning support programs within international schools is a positive shift. However, this progress is not enough. Every child has a right to education and every school should be equipped and willing to provide this. Whether it's a change in policy, acquiring more resources, or transforming viewpoints, the international education community must strive for inclusivity. This would ensure that every child, regardless of their learning needs, can receive the education they deserve without the fear of rejection. The process may be challenging, but the end goal – an international education landscape that truly celebrates diversity and inclusivity – is undoubtedly worth striving for.

Reflection Questions

1 **Perspective Reflection**: Considering the dual perspective of the author, both as a parent and a special educator, how does this unique position influence the depth and understanding of the challenges faced by families transitioning between schools internationally? How might this narrative differ if only told from one viewpoint?
2 **Moral Dilemma**: Elizabeth's journey through eight schools highlights the significant challenges faced by families with special needs children in the international school system. Reflect on the choices parents have to make regarding disclosure: is it always ethically right to be completely forthcoming in an application, given the potential negative consequences for the child? When might it be justifiable to withhold certain information for the betterment of the child?
3 **Comparison to National Systems**: How do the challenges faced by parents seeking education for their children with special needs in international settings compare to those in national or public-school systems, based on your knowledge? How do the legal and ethical obligations differ between the two contexts?
4 **Broader Implications**: Using Table 12.1 as a reference reflects on the larger societal implications of these challenges. What does this dichotomy between school and family points of view suggest about our global understanding and value of inclusive education? How can international schools be encouraged to adopt a more inclusive approach, and what might be the consequences if they don't?

13 Navigating Mistrust
Presume Competence

Written by Lori

> The next chapter was written by a parent who is also a teacher. Her insights emphasize the importance of trust, understanding, and collaboration between parents and educators, particularly when working with children with special needs. Drawing on personal experiences and insights, the authors aim to bridge the gap between families and professionals by stressing the importance of understanding, communication, and mutual respect. The intended audience for this chapter is parents, educators, and other professionals in the field, with a focus on fostering open communication and empathy for the benefit of the child.

Before Braden's official diagnosis of autism and intellectual developmental delay (IDD), he was assessed through our state's Child Find program. Child Find is a component of IDEA (Individuals with Disabilities Education Act) that requires states to identify, locate, and evaluate all resident children with disabilities, from birth to age 21, who need special education services (OAR 581-015-2080).

At age three, although they didn't have a name for it (a formal diagnosis), they determined he was "developmentally delayed," so he qualified for summer school programming through the school district. My husband, Mike, and I were both teachers and felt well versed in what constituted good teaching. So, when we first met Braden's summer school teachers, we were less than impressed.

When we picked him up after his first day, the speech language pathologist (SLP) came up to us with a bright smile and gleefully showed us that she had shown Braden two tiny pictures – one of cookies and one of carrots – and Braden picked cookies. Mike and I looked at each other with confusion. We had no idea why this was so important to this woman. They were not even real pictures, just black outline drawings of the food. And we were thinking, "Well, of course, he picked the cookies. Duh!"

These interactions between the SLP and us happened daily and Mike and I became increasingly frustrated. Why on earth was this so important to her? What a colossal waste of our son's time. Why wasn't she teaching him how to speak? That is what he needed to learn.

But we never asked.

We never asked because we were completely overwhelmed with life, our son's behaviors, and the complexities of his non-diagnosis of "developmental delay." What did that even mean?

DOI: 10.4324/9781032634357-16

We did not understand that this SLP was using PECS (Picture Exchange Communication System), a relatively common and scientifically backed program based on BF Skinner's work. It supports children and adults affected by various cognitive, physical, and communication challenges by using visual pictures to support their communication. Teaching PECS with fidelity involves a complicated and nuanced training program and comes with a steep financial component for practitioners. Not all teachers or therapists who use PECS have completed the demanding process and become certified. It is essential they have a solid foundation in understanding the implementation of the system. There are many phases, and each phase is dependent upon the previous. Skipping phases means skipping essential learning components for the individual, which could cause significant gaps.

As trained educators, Mike and I had never seen this before, so we assumed his SLP did not know what she was doing. In fact, she was implementing a program that she presumed, based on her background and training, would benefit our son.

When Braden was nine, I went to PECS training. It is an incredible program and is something I wish all special educators and families of children with communication difficulties could learn. Our son has had limited success using the program, but I have witnessed countless others learn to communicate successfully through the system and it has changed their lives for the better.

Interestingly enough, several years after we assumed that Braden's teachers were incompetent for introducing this communication system to him, I had a similar experience as a teacher when the SLP and I introduced this to a student with whom we were working. Ling* came to our program with no verbal language. It soon became apparent that she was an extremely bright young girl who had no way to communicate with others. So, we introduced her first to Proloquo2Go, an assistive communication program based on PECs and used on an iPad.

Ling excelled with this program. Soon, she was sharing stories about her weekend with us.

"I went to watch baseball. I ate popcorn. I drank Coke. Mom laughed."

The speech pathologist and I were over the moon at her success with this program. Each day we would meet and share stories of Ling's communication. We were excited – until we met with the family for an IEP meeting. When we shared this news with her family, their response took our breath away.

"We took the iPad away from Ling. We don't want her using this. She should be learning how to talk, and this is a waste of her time."

Devastated by this decision, we pleaded with the family to understand that Ling was communicating and that was the important thing. We told them we would continue to pair verbal language and speech therapy exercises with her functional communication lessons using the assistive device, but they refused. They told us they did not want us to continue with these lessons.

Exasperated, I finally asked Ling's mother if she had ever lost her voice. She had. I then asked her how that made her feel. She responded, "I was frustrated because I couldn't get what I wanted or needed." I then asked her how she thought Ling must have felt when she lost her voice, which is essentially what had happened when the iPad, her method of communication, was taken away from her.

That was the "aha" moment for Ling's mother. Ling had functional communication using her augmentative and alternative communication (AAC) device and that communication was her voice. It needed to be valued just as much as verbal communication. Ling's mother made that connection and agreed to continue to allow Ling to use her AAC for future communication.

We should note that there are multiple forms of AAC, including low-tech options such as writing, gestures and facial expressions, spelling words by pointing to a letter board, pointing to photos or written words, and sign language. Some high-tech options include using an app on an iPad or using a computer with a built-in voice (ASHA, *Augmentative*, AAC).

Experiencing this scenario as both parent and teacher opened my world a bit. There are several reasons why parents may be a bit hesitant to accept new methods and reticent in trusting their child's teacher/therapist. Many parents have had a history that most wouldn't naturally consider. They have been advocating for their child since birth. I've spoken with countless families who knew there was an issue with their child's development early on, only to be scoffed at by their pediatricians. They heard responses such as "Stay off the internet. He's fine." "Don't compare him to his sibling," and "He'll learn to speak when ready."

It can be highly frustrating as a parent to have your concerns brushed off as if they are unimportant or even real. Eventually, the families get a diagnosis and they're angry because they could have received support and therapy for their child much earlier.

Parents may have been treated poorly by a teacher or therapist in the past. As much as we want to believe that all teachers and therapists are excellent, we know that a handful of poorly trained ones out there give the whole profession a bad name. If a parent has had experience with one of these individuals, it may take an exceptionally long time to learn to trust a new person working with their child.

However, parents should presume that the professionals working with their child are competent. After our experience with PECS during those first few weeks of Braden's school career, Mike and I decided that we would enter new situations with an open mind. We also decided to trust the people who worked with Braden and assume they were competent in their respective fields. This trust made the school years much easier for all of us. We believed in the professionals who worked with our son and we saw results.

Occasionally, some of these individuals gave us reason to question their methods or intentions. So, we approached these situations calmly and respectfully by asking clarifying questions and seeking to understand. Throughout Braden's entire school career, we only had two individuals who we believed did not have Braden's best interest at the heart of their teaching. As we moved around and encountered many professionals throughout his life, this is an encouraging statistic.

I have heard multiple times in my lifetime that I am too trusting of people, that I should not immediately trust them, and that people should have to earn my trust. I feel the opposite. Believing in people and knowing they will do their best is a much healthier option. I highly encourage families navigating the school system to start with trust and presume competence.

Our own experience as teachers taught us that special educators and therapists are highly trained in their fields and continue to learn as a requirement of their profession. In our case, we became detectives whenever we encountered a new therapist or teacher. We asked questions, and the more questions we asked, the more faith we had in the people working with our son.

While higher education doesn't automatically translate to expertise in the field, let's examine the qualifications needed for various professionals within a multidisciplinary team. We can only attest to regulations in the United States, which have strict guidelines and qualifications; however, these types of qualifications are often used abroad (Table 13.1).

Recommended Strategies and Solutions

Be Open

Whether we are parents, educators, or therapists, we must be open and seek to understand. When we assume we know best, we are not open to learning. When we are not open to learning, we get stuck, and that does not benefit anyone.

Be a Detective

Parents, what can you do to help understand what your child is learning in their classroom or therapy center? Be a detective. Ask questions. Despite being overwhelmed and busy, do the research and learn about the methods and systems used. It will reduce your anxiety about your child's learning and help you understand the teaching or therapeutic strategies.

To make this more tangible for you, Table 13.2 shows an example of what I have used in the past to collect information about programs being used in my son's schools.

Whether we are parents, educators, or therapists, we must be open and seek to understand. When we assume we know best, we are not open to learning. When we are not open to learning, we get stuck, and that does not benefit anyone.

Table 13.1 Requirements for Various Special Education Professionals

	Special Ed Teacher	SLP	OT	Psychologist
Bachelor's Degree	Required	Required	Required	Required
Master's Degree	N/A 46% of Special Educators in the USA hold a MA	Required	Required	N/A
PhD	Optional	Optional	Optional	Required
Internship or Practicum	One to two years post BA (unpaid)	One year fellowship	One to two years post BA	4 years Internship during training program, one year pre-doc, sometimes additional postdoc years (depending on state)
Examinations	PRAXIS – Special education PRAXIS – Severe to Profound Needs	PRAXIS – Speech therapy comprehensive exams in university	National Board for Certification in Occupational Therapy	Examination in the Professional Practice of Psychology (EPPP) and State law exam (e.g., Juris Prudence)
Certifications/License	Depending on the state. Standard Teaching Credential + Special Education Endorsement (General, Hearing, Visual Impairment, etc.)	Certificate of Clinical Competence in Speech-Language Pathology (CCC-SLP)	Occupational Therapy License	Psychology License (state specific)

Table 13.2 Examples for Data Gathering

Student Challenge	Program Used	Short Description	Research to Support Program
Communication	iPad–Proloquo2go	Speak. Proloquo2Go is an easy-to-use communication app for people who cannot speak or have articulation difficulties. Featuring natural sounding voices, including real children's voices, Proloquo2Go is a simple yet powerful AAC	"The role of augmentative and alternative communication for children with autism: current status and future trends" https://www.ncbi.nlm.nih.gov/pmc/articles/PMC5036660/
Social Skills	The Zones of Regulation	The Zones of Regulation creates a systematic approach to teach regulation by categorizing all the diverse ways we feel and states of alertness we experience into four concrete-colored zones. (Kuyper, *Learn more about the zones*, 2021)	Evidence & The Zones of Regulation https://www.zonesofregulation.com/research--evidence-base.html

This chapter is not simply for parents. To teachers, psychologists, and therapists working with a child – please, please, please presume competence and positive intentions of the parents. To let you in on a little secret: parents know their kids. And we need to listen to them and try to understand their perspective.

You might be thinking, "But Lori, you just described an entire scenario where you and your husband obviously didn't know that PECS was best for your son." And you are right. We did not. But that does not mean we don't know our son. We simply did not understand the *why* of the speech pathologist's methods. Once we understood them, we backed the program a hundred percent.

So, here is an example of us knowing our son. Now that Braden is an adult, he is in multiple programs in our state. For these programs, there is often an interview process with many meetings. As Braden is 22, he needs to attend all the meetings. As his legal guardians, we told the organizers of these meetings numerous times that Braden should not participate. He gets distraught when people talk about him, whether positive or negative. He abhors it, which he makes clear when, during a meeting, he might a) tear apart his clothing, b) self-harm by picking at his skin, or even c) wet his pants. Why, as his advocates, would we want to put him through that?

The very well-intentioned groups organizing the meetings do not understand our reluctance to have Braden attend these meetings. After all, if we're making decisions for him, he should be there. I mean, it makes sense. But here it is. WE KNOW OUR SON. We know this is not good for him. We know it hurts his heart and he shows us this by demonstrating behaviors. So, despite our advocating, they mandated his attendance at the meetings. However, once he began showing the behaviors, the groups changed their minds and told us he did not need to attend. In the end, they did what was best for Braden, but wouldn't it have been easier if they had just listened to the people who knew him best in this world at the very beginning?

So, I will repeat what I wrote earlier in this chapter:

Be Open

Whether we are parents, educators, or therapists, we must be open and seek to understand. When we assume we know best, we are not open to learning. When we are not open to learning, we get stuck, which does not benefit anyone.

Part of being open is knowing that we need to meet parents where they are and never assume they do not have expertise in the area.

Be Understanding

As we work with families, we must understand that they all come with their own school histories and may have questions about our methods when working with their children. We need to realize that they may not have the same schema as we do. While our curriculum and methods make complete sense to us, they might be extremely confusing to them.

While time is always a precious commodity when teaching, sharing your methods and the philosophy behind them builds bridges and helps parents understand the "why." Once the "why" is understood, trust is built.

We need to meet parents where they are and never assume they do not have expertise in the area. However, many parents do know the why. They come with years of learning about their child and understand the programs that work best for them.

I interviewed Jon Springer, a father of two neurodiverse children. Jon is just one parent of many who shared their frustrations with me about how they do not feel heard at meetings about their children. Jon recalled his frustration when working with some educators and therapists in the past:

> I have found the following does not matter in my parent-teacher interactions as a parent: having a Master's in Teaching in Elementary Ed and English Language Acquisition, that I've sat online through 4 years of

speech therapy, that I spent 18 months doing OT online as an OT assistant, that I've sacrificed career & self to spend time with my kids & intervene, that we hired an education specialist to train us hands-on to improve our interactions with our kids four weeks a year for 3 1/2 years. And, that's okay. The most ridiculous thing of all is having to prove as a parent that you know your child. ... Every. Single. Year. Doubly or triply so when you switch schools. Every year, at every parent-teacher conference, words have to be chosen wisely, critiques or suggestions have to be chosen very carefully. Every step for those of us parents who KNOW, we know every utterance has to strategically relationship-build to get the best outcomes for our child.

Teachers spend years studying to become great at their craft. They have ongoing professional development requirements few professions have. At issue: Are teachers confident enough in their expertise that they don't need to mark their territory as a bear does its forest territory? Can we coexist in a space of expertise where parent knowledge of the child and teacher pedagogical knowledge unite as partners, as collaborators in student triumph?

Can we coexist in a space of expertise where parent knowledge of the child and teacher pedagogical knowledge unite as partners, as collaborators in student triumph?
—Jon Springer, Parent

Be a Teacher

As an educator or therapist, teaching doesn't end with our students. Take time to explain the programs to families. We cannot presume that our families know or understand the theory and practice of our therapies. By taking the time to explain it and provide the research behind it, we begin to build the foundation of trust. Families may have many questions or just a few, but it is essential to answer them all. Families need to feel heard as they may have had past experiences where they were not.

Be Compassionate

Teaching special education is difficult. Between all the paperwork, ensuring we are meeting our state or government regulations, working with families, working with administration (who may or may not be supportive of our programs), collaborating with general education teachers, training our assistants, building a team, and planning individualized lessons for our students, it can be quite overwhelming. In fact, as a teacher, I know that it can be so overwhelming, and sometimes we are so busy and exhausted that compassion for other people's situations can be hard to come by.

As a parent, I know that we crave compassion from our child's team of educators. We do not always share what is happening at home as we fear judgment. I have heard teachers talking about parents in the staff room. "Why don't they just …?" fill in the blanks. Whenever I hear it, my heart breaks because judgment is the last thing families need.

My son, profoundly impacted by his autism, cannot communicate his sadness or frustration. He sometimes gets violent with the people he loves the most – us, his parents. There were many times I sent Braden off to school after he either bit me or pulled chunks of hair out of my head and I did not say a word.

You might be wondering why I didn't tell the school. Some answers: shame, fear, embarrassment, and judgment. One time I told the teacher that Braden had bitten me that morning. Her reply? "Why don't you just bite him back? That will teach him."

Well, first of all. No, that won't "teach him." And second, why was she judging my parenting? It made me question her overall attitude toward my son. If he demonstrated a behavior at school, would she punish him rather than try to help him?

She wasn't the only teacher who judged me when I shared. Once, I mentioned that Braden didn't sleep most evenings. A teacher suggested that I give him a better bedtime routine so he would have to sleep. There was no empathy, just a suggestion, which we had previously tried to no avail. She could have asked what his evening routine was *before* telling me to create one. She could have told me about her child's poor sleep and how they were able to fix it, but instead, she assumed we did not have a solid bedtime routine in place. She assumed she knew better than I did. So, I stopped sharing it altogether. And that didn't help anyone.

I cannot stress enough how important it is to be compassionate. Family members are caregivers and we, as educators, may have no idea what is going on behind closed doors. So, we need to assume that our families are doing the absolute best they can at any one time.

We also need to understand that:

- There is no such thing as relaxing when you have a child with severe needs. Parents are exhausted as they give 150% all day and all night. Many work full time and then start their next full-time job once they have returned home.

- Parents love their child more than anything. They celebrate the positives with pure joy, while each negative event hits them like a ton of bricks. It is emotionally crushing. Sometimes those highs and lows hit in the same week, the same day, or even the same hour.
- Parents have made so many sacrifices for their children. Therapies and private schools (if necessary) are expensive. Many gave up good jobs, as the country or school district they moved to could not support their child's needs. But they do what they must to ensure their child receives the best care possible.
- Many students experience significant sleep disorders, which means their parents do not sleep either. Sleep deficiency is known to cause memory loss, susceptibility to illness, and many more health issues (Mcbean & Schlosnagle, 2016).

Compassionate educators ask parents what they need. They ask to hear about the behaviors happening in the home so that they can work on those skills in the classroom. Rather than telling parents what they should be doing, they collaborate with the parents to design plans and systems that support everyone involved.

Compassionate educators listen to families. They do not judge and they certainly don't gossip about them in the teacher workroom.

Be Communicative

One straightforward way to have parents share information is using a back-and-forth book. Whether it is electronic or paper, it really does not matter. The point is all in the name: back-and-forth.

Here is a sample of one I used in the past. This one is simplistic, and you can get similar ones on Teachers Pay Teachers (TPT) and customize them for your classroom. It is simple, as it shares what the child did during the day at school and has a personalized note from the teacher to communicate about unique events or even some behaviors shown throughout the day (Figure 13.1).

The power comes in the parent note. Families of my students filled it out in the morning before school. They communicated if their child slept or not or if anything happened the evening before that we should know. They also shared fun information, such as going out to a restaurant or visiting the zoo. This communication provided me with what I needed to know to start the day. If the child didn't sleep, I was more understanding when they needed to take a rest during the day or had trouble regulating their emotions. I also used what they did the evening before as conversation starters at circle time. If the child was nonverbal, I quickly printed out some icons or prepared their AAC device. Hence, they had the opportunity to communicate with me about their adventures from the evening before.

Back-and-forth books are a highly effective method of communication for all parties. Our occupational therapist and SLP filled out the booklet on days

Figure 13.1 Daily Communication Log Example

when they worked with the student as well, so the parents had a clear picture of what the day looked like for their child. As students get older and more proficient with communication, they can take ownership of the back-and-forth book by filling out the activities they did that day and how they felt their day was overall. It opens up an easy way for parents and children to communicate with one another rather than simply asking, "How was school today?"

In the end, whether we are parents, therapists, or teachers, it's all about having positive presuppositions about one another. If we can be open to learning as teachers, parents, and therapists and be communicative, compassionate, understanding, and collaborative, we can begin to bridge the gaps that past experiences may have created.

Reflection Question

1 Considering the depth of experiences and knowledge both parents and teachers bring to the table, how can educators create a space where both parental understanding of their child and the pedagogical expertise of teachers are recognized and respected, fostering a true collaboration for the success of the student?

14 Navigating Professional Relationships

I've Been Teaching Longer Than You've Been Alive, Honey

Written by Psychologist in Training (e.g., Amanda)

The next chapter is a story narrated by a student en route to obtaining their doctorate. It is written for consultants, educators, graduate students, and professionals within the field and emphasizes the dynamics of professional relationships, particularly between those with different levels of experience, and offers insights on collaboration and mutual respect.

As part of the training program, we needed to do a fair amount of research. One of the long-term studies I was involved in during graduate school included consulting with teachers in the public schools in Baton Rouge, Louisiana. As part of this consultation, we needed to ask the teachers a standard set of questions that included background information on the teacher – how long they had been in the field, and so on. I will never forget one of my first assignments in one of the public schools in Baton Rouge when I started working with a seasoned teacher. She saw me (a bright-eyed, 20-something graduate student) walking into her classroom to *help* her. So, when I asked her how long she had been teaching, it should probably have come as no surprise that she replied in a very snarky way, "Oh, longer than you've been alive, honey." She may or may not have said honey, but the tone said it all. She was not keen on these graduate school types walking into her classroom – her world – to tell her what to do.

Needless to say, when that is the way a consultation starts, I am not sure how effective it is going to be. Even if you do everything by the books and adhere to all the best practices, *nothing matters if you cannot connect the relationship*. Yet, there is very little research on this area or attention to this seemingly unimportant yet crucial detail. I don't remember the nuance of that case or assignment, nor do I remember the outcome. Still, it did tune me into a chronic problem within consultation – the relationship you have with the consultant/consultee matters. If either party is unwilling to see each person's value to the relationship, then it is unlikely you will have a productive or positive outcome. I found this theme commonplace through the early part of my career, especially among the more senior, tenured educators. There was a sense of *what can this young person who has not experienced the things that I have experienced bring to the table.* How often I got suspicious looks and loaded questions:

"How old ARE you?" or "Oh, YOU'RE the doctor?" or "Do you even have kids of your own?" It was as if, somehow, I could not offer anything if I did not answer their questions correctly. Like somehow, I could not be respected or maybe even trusted if I gave the wrong answers.

If either party is unwilling to see the value that each person brings to the relationship, then it is unlikely you will have a productive or positive outcome.

As someone who is now later in their career, I understand the inherent mistrust of youth when it comes to solving problems in their space, their arena. I understand that *this person cannot understand my world if they haven't ever had children of their own or if they have not experienced the things that I have*, even though I have been on the receiving end of that mistrust. It's hard to articulate how to deal with this problem or how to make it better. I remember adopting the mindset that I would just "do me" and stay steady; over time, I would win them over when they saw the "proof in the pudding." Even with this approach, you still can't win 'em all.

I also remember a helpful way to gain credibility when talking with resistant teachers was to remind them that even though I didn't have children of my own, I felt like I'd had hundreds of children by working with the students and clients I had. Often, the kids that I see are labeled as the "worst of the worst" or the kids that are tough to reach. These are not my words and are very inappropriate but that was a phrase I often heard about students who other providers were unable to support. Although I didn't have children of my own at the time, it *felt* as if I had many children. I treated each and every client as if they were my own. How would I like my child treated, what would I like my child to be working on, what goals would I want for my child, and what were the barriers that I could help them overcome?

I remember feeling very inadequate early on when people would put me on the defensive by asking these sorts of questions. Like I needed to jump through these invisible hoops to prove just how competent I was, with or without having kids of my own. In fact, because I went to graduate school, I delayed my own family life and didn't yet have my first child. Until I had children of my own, I wanted to work with the "worst of the worst," the kids that no one could reach, the "hopeless" or those that "were beyond reach." I took a lot of pride in seeking out these kids and made it my mission to reach them, affect them, and impact them. The sense of meaning and pride that I got from this work was powerful. It is one thing to do what you do and affects typical kids or common problems; it is an entirely different thing when you reach the "unreachable" student. The impact when you see that what you do has a positive effect on a child is a joy unlike any other I have ever had. It is something that will still bring me to tears to this day, thinking about those moments throughout my career.

Whether you are new in your career or seasoned as a therapist, psychologist, physician, or any other childhood consultant – if you want to be an effective consultant, you MUST find a way to join the existing team of people who are already working with this student. Do not just go in and start pushing your point of view or way on the existing team. Do not assume you know how to "fix" the situation. Certainly, don't start doling out advice before actually getting a feel for what is going on. Take the time to understand what was attempted in the past and what worked and did not. An essential part of the consultation process is to LISTEN authentically. The existing team of professionals (parents included) will most certainly pick up on inauthentic listening or inadvertent patronizing. So, do everyone a favor – take the time to listen and get to know the situation before trying to add your input.

An important part of the consultation process [as a Psychologist] is to authentically LISTEN. This needs to occur straight away and cannot be phoned in.

Include the teacher/parent/coach/co-treating therapist in the assessment, diagnostic, and treatment process. Ask them questions and immediately acknowledge that they bring enormous insight about the child and the history of the problem. The only way to be successful in teaching and learning is to include those who are with the child day in and day out. Interventions only have long-term effectiveness when carried out by those who surround the child on a regular basis. Additionally, a consultant is only as good as the information they have. The best, most accurate information is obtained from experts on the child, mainly because consultants are only with the child for a brief period. For the consultation to be helpful, both parties must collaborate on behalf of the child. Sometimes what the consultant brings to the table is a fresh perspective simply because they are not close to the problem on a daily basis. Sometimes, that is all you need to get a problem unstuck; however, nothing positive is likely to occur without the ability to establish mutual respect and create a collaborative team.

> *Nothing a consultant does will have any long-term effects unless it is continued to be carried out by those who surround the child on a regular basis.*

In conclusion, the journey from a fresh-eyed graduate student to a seasoned professional in consultation work is a complex road marked by challenges, discoveries, and profound fulfillment. It is a journey wherein humility, patience, and genuine respect for others' experiences become indispensable tools. An effective consultant must tread lightly, imbibe the wisdom offered by the existing team, and harness the power of collaborative teamwork. While the work can sometimes be met with mistrust and resistance, the chance to positively impact a child's life makes every hurdle worthwhile. It is essential to remember that our role as consultants is not to "fix" problems single-handedly but to join an existing community of caregivers in finding effective, sustainable solutions. As consultants, our unique advantage is our ability to provide fresh perspectives, but we must never forget that our insights are only as good as the information we gather and our ability to listen authentically. The strength of the consultant–consultee relationship is central to making a lasting impact, requiring that we appreciate the nuances of the situation, respect the history of efforts, and collaborate intensely with those who know the child best. The goal is not to always win them over but to foster a shared sense of purpose in nurturing the child's development.

Reflection Questions

1 **Importance of Relationships in Consultation**: The chapter emphasizes the pivotal role of relationships in the field of consultation. Reflect on a time when you felt dismissed or unvalued because of your age or experience level. How did it affect your ability to communicate, and what strategies could be employed to bridge such gaps in professional relationships?

2 **Valuing Experience and Knowledge**: Considering the story narrated by the author, in what ways can seasoned professionals balance their acquired wisdom with openness to new perspectives, and how can newer entrants in the field honor the experience of veterans while contributing their unique insights?
3 **Active Listening as a Skill**: The author mentions the importance of "authentic listening." What do you understand by this term, and how does it differ from general listening? Can you recall a moment where authentic listening made a difference in your professional or personal life?
4 **Collaborative Approaches**: Based on the concluding section of the chapter, reflect on the statement: "The strength of the consultant–consultee relationship is central to making a lasting impact." In what ways have you seen collaboration lead to more significant positive outcomes in your own experiences, and how can one actively promote a more collaborative approach in professional settings?

15 Navigating Through Misguided Notions
Golden Ticket

Written by Lori

The chapter that follows is written from the dual perspective of a parent and teacher of a child with special needs. It targets parents, teachers, and professionals, focusing on dispelling misconceptions about special education and emphasizing individualized support for children with disabilities.

I write a blog about life with my son, Braden. Most of the time, my blog centers around raising him and some of the trials, tribulations, and celebrations we have. I've shared a few of these blog posts throughout this book. They tend to capture the essence of what we want for the reader experience: understanding the point of view of everyone on the student's team is not only important but also critical.

(Blog Post Written 2018)

I'm sure you've read or have seen the movie *Charlie and the Chocolate Factory*. Can't you just see Charlie skipping down the street and singing the magical song once he found a winning chocolate bar? He got the golden ticket. He gets to go and visit Willy Wonka's chocolate factory. He can have anything he wants now.

What you may not know is that apparently, kids with special needs have won golden tickets too. I mean, I didn't realize this – until today.

I belong to a Facebook group for special educators. It's a fantastic group. People ask questions regarding strategies, curriculums, IEPs, how to handle tricky situations, and so on. People chime in and help when they can. It's been a great support to me this year. I like it because it never really gets contentious and people are incredibly respectful.

Until today …

A special needs educator posted because she was getting pushback from parents who were upset that she (the teacher) was failing their son, who is in kindergarten. The teacher explained that the boy doesn't know his letters or recognize his name as well as some other things, which thereby means he should fail kindergarten. She thinks it's only fair to fail the boy as he is, after all, not meeting kindergarten standards. She said, "We all know that he has the 'golden ticket' to graduate anyway."

I wrote back, "I'm confused. Are you saying that because this boy has special needs, he has a golden ticket?"

"Yes, everyone in our district knows these kids have a golden ticket for graduation."

"To clarify, you mean kids with special needs?" I asked.

"Yes."

WHAT?

Okay, there are so many things wrong with this sentiment. It's hard to explain it all, but I want to try. Students with disabilities in the United States are entitled to the least restrictive environment (LRE). This means that they should be in a setting where they can access the curriculum with the least amount of support they need.

So, it sounds like this boy has a documented special need and he will fail kindergarten because of placement in the wrong setting. From her description, he has a developmental delay, which means his development is delayed. So, if he isn't reading his name or recognizing letters, it makes sense because he is not developmentally ready to do so. Think about a 2- or 3-year-old. Most of them are not doing these things either. It's okay because their brains are not developmentally there yet.

Let's say you were in an accident and were in a coma for two years. You came out and were then placed in the grade level as your same-aged peers. But you missed two whole years of education. You wouldn't be able to function at grade level. Should you fail, or should you be provided with instruction to help you fill in the gaps?

Anyway, this boy needs a different placement, one where he can work on the areas he needs to work on without the fear of failure. He shouldn't be in a kindergarten classroom full time with the expectation that he learns exactly what his peers are learning. He needs an IEP tailored to his specific needs.

I asked this person, "Do you just keep retaining the boy until he can recognize his letters?"

She responded, "He should fail kindergarten."

Braden still does not know his letters. Braden does not know his numbers. He can't identify his name. He's 18 years old (at the time of this blog post).

Apparently, he should never have made it past kindergarten.

Now let's explore the "Golden Ticket" theory.

Imagine this scenario. You are a parent. You have a beautiful baby. That baby is perfect in every way. Then you notice that he is not developing like his sister. He is not speaking. He is not communicating. He is not pointing or interacting with you. You go to the doctor. She tells you your son has autism. Severe autism.

So, you ... CELEBRATE!!! Pop the champagne. Hallelujah, this is awesome! My son has just won a Golden Ticket for graduation. Hot dog. I never win anything, and I just got the biggest prize of them all!

I want to challenge anyone who feels this way to spend one day – heck, one hour – in the shoes of a parent or a child living with special learning needs.

Is it golden when:

1. Your child can't communicate, so they scream, melt down, and pull your hair in front of a group of strangers?
2. Your child melts down in a grocery store and the clerk tells you that your child is spoiled?
3. Your child opens a window on the second floor, throws out all of his sibling's awards and trophies, and smashes them to bits?
4. Your child throws two computers and three iPads out of a window?
5. Your child is so sad but can't communicate why, so just sits and cries for days?
6. Your child learns some letters one day and an hour later cannot remember them, points to his head and says, "I not know"?
7. You must still clean up after your adult child when he uses the bathroom?
8. You haven't slept in weeks because your child has a sleep disorder that keeps him up all night long?
9. Your child has never even had one friend?
10. You stop getting invited out because people are uncomfortable around your child?

I can answer. It's not so golden.

Don't get me wrong. I love my son. I love our life. I just ask you not to minimize the long road that families with special needs must go along. We do it out of love. Most do it with little complaint, but when we hear people tell us that somehow our kids have it easy ...

Because they get to graduate even though they don't know their ABCs? Truly absurd.

Our kids with special learning needs must work a hundred times harder to learn the same thing typically developing children learn easily. Nothing comes easy for them or their parents.

Rather than worry about this child taking the easy route to high school graduation, I vote we worry about how we can help him and his family get everything he needs now to learn and to grow and to be happy – now – at age five. Help his family understand that learning will take him longer than his peers. Teach him what he needs to learn. Maybe he will never learn his letters or sounds. But he can still learn to read. Teach him how to brush his teeth, how to walk safely across a busy intersection, and how to stay quiet in a library or a movie theater. He can learn. He may need to learn different things than his peers.

In other words, teach him. Don't fail him.

Our kids may be able to graduate from high school without knowing the things their peers know. But does that mean they can live on their own someday? Can they get a job? Will they have a family?

I do believe that life is golden – but all our paths and journeys are different. May we all learn to respect each other and understand that when we pick up our tickets to start our big trip, we don't know which we will get. So, may we care for those who might have to stop at more places to get to their ultimate destination and never assume they somehow got off easy because they got a ticket they didn't even get to choose.

Reflection Questions

1 In this chapter, Lori challenges the notion that a "Golden Ticket" is a privilege, using specific examples of the challenges faced by her son. Can you identify any prejudices or misconceptions you or someone you know might have held about individuals with special needs?
2 How can this blog post inspire or inform us, as educators or therapists, in our approach toward working with children who have special learning needs and their families? What changes, if any, would you consider implementing in your practice after reading this?

16 Navigating Different Schools of Thought
Old School Versus New School

Written Dr. Ly

> *The following chapter is written from an expert's perspective, contrasting traditional and modern approaches in teaching and psychology. It is aimed at professionals and educators in these fields, emphasizing adaptation and the importance of staying updated with current research and practices.*

Over time, I have developed my own personal theory of what makes a therapist/teacher/practitioner of a particular discipline successful or not. This theory identifies individuals from various fields who are "old school" versus "new school." At first, I used to apply this theory to teachers only but began to see it across a multitude of other disciplines (i.e., various therapists, applied behavior analysts, physicians).

I began connecting the dots between effective teachers and ineffective teachers and attaching modern language (at the time, just in my head) to the data. In essence, the teachers who were willing to *adapt* and *modify* what they were doing to fit the students' needs were classified (in my mind) as "new school" versus those unwilling/unable to adapt and modify what they were doing to meet their needs, who I describe as "old school" [of thought]. Old-school educators do things the way they do them, the way they've always done them, and it is the child who needs to adjust or adapt to THEIR WAY. If the child does not "get it," it is their fault, and they "did their best." In contrast, a new-school educator recognizes that many students learn differently and will implement a multitiered approach to instruction and provide modifications suited to each student.

> *Old School [of thought] expects the student to adapt and adjust to their way of teaching versus New School, who adapts and adjusts their teaching methods to meet the needs of the student.*

There is nothing inherently wrong with old school, just that it is an outdated notion that better teaching methods have replaced. I am not blaming old-school teachers and in fact, many of them are incredible at what they do and have been successful with many of their students. My point in bringing up this distinction is to take notice of the latest research and continue to evolve the practice of educating (and all disciplines) as the literature suggests current best practice.

Old school does NOT mean "old person" as plenty of young teachers were trained in subpar programs or never received the "new school" training. Old school is an outdated school of thought, NOT an old person!

> *Old school [of thought] does NOT mean "old person" as there are plenty of young teachers who were trained in subpar programs or who never received the "new school" training. Old school is an outdated school of thought, NOT an old person!*

When I began practicing internationally, I began to see more and more of how this "old school" versus "new school" applied to far more than just teachers and just how widespread it was. In essence, new school philosophy captures the HIGH QUALITY of care delivered by teachers, therapists (SLP, OT, PT, ABA, etc.), psychologists, and physicians. No one is immune to falling into the "old school" (low quality) trap. It happens when someone in whatever discipline they are in learns what they learn in school and then just stops learning. Or perhaps they keep up with continuing education requirements for a while but then decide they are specialized enough and stop there. It's easy to do, as you can imagine. Everyone is busy in their respective lives and careers. Research never ends. Keeping up with the latest research once you complete your formal education can seem overwhelming, but it is vital. When we don't keep up with the most current research or continue to strive to improve our quality of care, ultimately, it is the students we serve who suffer.

"Old School" versus "New School" [of thought] translates into quality of care that we deliver to those we serve. We must continue to strive to keep up with research best practices in order to deliver the highest quality of service and not get stuck in old ways of thinking.

As a self-proclaimed perfectionist, I HEAR YOU! It is not possible to keep up with *all of the research all of the time*. I do think that is not an excuse to do nothing. We need to check in with the literature about the key tenets of change as our careers progress. Continue going to conferences and reading professional journals, continue engaging in conversations with professionals in the field, and question our assumptions/practices. For sure, we need to remain open-minded and understand that the science of behavior is ever changing and we will always have much to learn.

Understand that this applies to far more than just teachers! NEWSFLASH: IT IS EVERYWHERE AND IN EVERY DISCIPLINE! The more time I spend out of school, in foreign countries, working with many disciplines, I see how ubiquitous this problem is.

The "quality of care" thing reaches far and wide.

I have seen it in psychologists, counselors, teachers, therapists (OT/SLP/ABA), physicians, nurses, and the list goes on and on. Okay, don't get dismayed; that does not mean we all need to be versed on best practices in all the preceding disciplines, just that we need to understand that quality of care is a thing and know what we can do about it.

Specifically, I will talk about something near and dear to me, the field of applied behavior analysis (ABA). Many of you reading this book will already have some (or many) feelings (good or bad) about ABA. For those of you who are not familiar, ABA is the practice of applying the psychological principles of learning theory in a systematic way to modify behavior. The practice is used most extensively in special education and the treatment of autism spectrum disorder (ASD), but also in healthcare, animal training, and even business. ABA is widely recognized as the most scientifically valid therapy available for treating behavioral issues associated with ASD (https://www.appliedbehavior analysisedu.org/what-is-aba/).

ABA's origins began with B.F. Skinner and Ivan Pavlov when they established early experimental analysis of behavior and the foundational key tenets of behaviorism but have evolved a lot since then. Current ABA is built on the foundations of Skinner/Pavlov's experimental analysis and has broadened behaviorism to become more "applied" and more relevant to modern human behavior. It is incredibly well researched and very well supported in the literature.

That said, ABA still has a bad rap, which gets me back on point: old school vs. new school. Old school practitioners technically use the tenets established by our founding fathers and utilize behavior principles. However (and it's a big however), they fail to implement any new research about how to adapt these tenants to meet current needs. Remember, old school does not adapt, new school does! Then you have world-class ABA practitioners doing new-school ABA and working magic with the kids they serve, yet the old-school folks sometimes bring the entire discipline down. I can't tell you how many times I've worked with teachers, schools, or colleagues who had a terrible view of ABA before I arrived. In essence, I had to rebrand ABA for them in order for them to see its value (and listen to anything that I said). These bad experiences will linger on and on. These individuals had a legitimate bad experience with an old-school practitioner and decided that it wasn't just a bad therapist, but it was ABA that was bad. Ugh – this is so frustrating when you know how much value a good therapist can bring to a kid or a family! If ABA isn't your thing, just insert what you do when I write those letters; insert teacher, therapist, psychologist, physician, or other. The individual delivering your service matters! A great deal, in fact.

> *You have world class ABA practitioners who are doing new-school ABA and working magic with the kids they serve, yet the old-school folks sometimes bring the entire discipline down.*

I attended a high-quality training program for ABA, which was well respected. I didn't even realize that ABA had a bad side (a dark side, if you will) until much later when I started traveling very far away. I distinctly remember glowing about it and having a parent/colleague sneer at me. I was shocked. Up to that point, nearly everyone I had been in touch with had had remarkable growth, progress, and experience and attributed it to the wonderful world of ABA. It was a rude awakening but an extremely important lesson. The world is full of mediocre or poor messengers of various disciplines, but it's up to the good ones not to let *them* define our profession.

> *The world is full of mediocre or poor messengers of various disciplines but it's up to the goods ones to not let them define [the] profession.*

Another example: I remember several times when I listened to accounts from my clients or questioned my co-treating physicians. I realized, *"holy smokes,"* not even medical doctors are immune to being old school if they don't keep up with best practices. Many examples shocked me, such as pediatricians who ignored major developmental delays and red flags, telling parents that "the child would grow out of it" or "just sit tight. It's just a phase." Conversely, rather than overlooking or not diagnosing, I have known several other pediatricians who would diagnose a child with conditions with scant evidence or solely based on parent account. Some have never even seen the child! Neither of these approaches is considered best practice.

> *The individual delivering your service (regardless of what that is) matters! Take the time to shop around and ask questions!*

    What to do about this now that you/we recognize keeping current with best practices across all disciplines is not a given and can be problematic? It is impossible for you to know about every discipline and read every professional journal. In the absence of that, my best advice is to ask questions. Always come with questions. Anyone that is competent in what they are doing and has the data to support it will easily be able to field questions. Parents, I do not suggest that you interrogate every therapist/teacher/physician who works with your child, but definitely ask questions. I often do meet-and-greet before ever working with anyone. Have a conversation with them, ask them simple questions, and have the conversation flow. Do this occasionally while working with someone and you will get a feel. If something feels off or wrong, ask more questions. Good professionals will either have answers for you or express the limits to their knowledge (this is another way to know they are good – ethics dictate NOT to practice outside your area of competence). It's a giant red flag if someone you are working with seems to have answers to everything about everything.

> *If something feels off or wrong [when working with someone], ask more questions. Good professionals will either have answers for you or will express the limits to their knowledge.*

In conclusion, the distinction between "old school" and "new school" is far more pervasive than just within the realm of teaching. It is indeed ubiquitous across many professions, affecting the quality of care we provide to our students, patients, or clients. As practitioners, it's essential that we consistently challenge our understanding, embrace lifelong learning, and remain adaptable to evolving best practices. Not doing so runs the risk of falling into an outdated "old school" mindset, which can potentially limit our ability to effectively serve those in our care. As parents or consumers of these services, it is essential to question, evaluate, and ensure that your service providers are abreast of the most recent research and methodologies in their fields. To maintain and elevate the quality of care, we must avoid complacency and continue to foster a culture of curiosity, growth, and adaptability. Always remember, the "new school" approach isn't just a trendy buzzword – it is a commitment to continuous improvement and the pursuit of excellence in our respective disciplines. It is about never settling, about always pushing for better, for ourselves and for those we serve.

Reflection Questions

1 **Personal Reflection on Practices**: Reflect on your own practice or profession. Are there moments or aspects where you recognize an "old school" mentality in your own methods or thought processes? How do these compare to newer, more adaptable methods you're aware of?
2 **Addressing Resistance to Change**: How can one effectively address resistance to change, especially when faced with professionals or colleagues who are deeply ingrained in the "old school" way of thinking? What strategies might be effective in promoting the value and necessity of continuous learning and adaptability?
3 **Impact of Quality Care**: Drawing from the examples in the chapter, what are the potential consequences for students or clients when service providers do not stay updated with best practices? Conversely, what benefits arise when professionals commit to a "new school" approach and prioritize current research and methodologies?
4 **Role of Feedback in Continuous Improvement**: How do feedback and reflection play a role in transitioning from an "old school" to a "new school" approach? In what ways can seeking feedback from peers, clients, or patients help professionals in ensuring they are providing the highest quality of care?

17 Navigating Bias

There's No Such Thing as a Lazy Kid

Written by Lori

> *The next chapter is written from an educator's perspective, challenging the notion of "lazy" students. Through personal experiences and expert insights, the author emphasizes empathy and collaboration. The target audience includes teachers, parents, and others involved in children's education, encouraging a more compassionate approach to perceived laziness.*

I want to share another blog post I wrote back in 2015. As the supporting team for our students, we (teachers, parents, and therapists) must believe in them.
(Lori's Blog Post, 2015)
I was sitting in a leadership meeting at a previous school I worked in, and we were discussing assessments and grading. Our school was standards based and had been for a while before I got there. This system is one reason I chose this school, as it aligned with my philosophy of education and assessment. Soon a debate began, and one of my colleagues said, "Well, what about the lazy kids? We're expected to put in all this work to make them do their assignments, but they're so lazy they don't do them."

There were a few nods in the room. Many of us sat there quietly. I was new to the school and did not believe I had the right to speak up. (I still regret this decision).

Here is what I wish I would have said:

Joe, I'm going to tell it to you straight now. There's no such thing as a lazy kid. Let me repeat that statement just in case you missed it: THERE'S NO SUCH THING AS A LAZY KID!

Phew! I feel better already. I just needed to get that out there.

Dr. Ross Greene, an American Clinical Psychologist and author of multiple books, including *The Explosive Child* and *Lost at School*, has worked for the past 20 years or more on changing the narrative that kids are lazy. I first picked up Dr. Greene's book *The Explosive Child* in 2001 when we noticed our son was not developing at the same rate as his peers, and he was having multiple meltdowns a day. The title spoke to me as my son's explosive behaviors were unexplainable.

As I read through this book, I soon understood that my son was having these meltdowns because he had no way of communicating his needs or wants. Dr. Greene's underlying themes are that "if kids could do well, they would do well" and "doing well is always preferable to not doing well (Greene, 2010a)."

Think of it this way. Have you ever tried something and not enjoyed it because it was hard? Did you persevere through it, or did you give up? Chances are, you've done both. I know I have. Why were you able to persist at times and give up the others? Motivation might have something to do with it, but more than likely, something was getting in the way of your learning that skill.

At one stage in my life, I decided I wanted to learn how to quilt. I needed a hobby, and many of my friends had taken it up, so I thought, "well, why not? I should be able to do this." Oh my. I overestimated my ability. You see, my entire life, I've struggled with fine motor skills. Untying a knot in my shoelace is difficult for me. Quilting required me to thread needles and sew in straight lines. My small quilt sat unfinished for many months, and every single time I thought about attempting it again, I realized how difficult it was for me. I had no desire to continue. It was too challenging and not enjoyable!

Not only did I make this discovery about my son from reading this book, but it was a light-bulb moment for me as an educator as well. As a Grade 4 teacher at the time, I had many students who I labeled as "lazy" or "unmotivated." They just wouldn't do the work. I made my lessons engaging and fun, so why wouldn't they do it? I couldn't understand until I read this book. Dr. Greene explained that if you ascribe to the philosophy that *kids do well if they can* as opposed to *kids do well if they want to do well*, then you as an educator or as a parent can actually do something about it. In fact, you do what is needed to ensure that the child does well. If you believe that a child is inherently lazy, there is absolutely nothing you can do to help that child except give them a consequence, which ultimately does not change the behavior. Alternatively, if you believe that a child does well, if they can do well, then you can move forward. Ask yourself this question. What is the underlying issue? Is it a past or current trauma? Is it a learning challenge of some sort? Is it sensory related?

Now I'm going to share a story that I'm not particularly proud of, but hopefully, it sheds some light on this philosophy.

At one time in my life, I worked at a prestigious and high-achieving middle school. My role was to work with students who were not meeting the standards and support them as needed. I had a student who I shall call Paul. Paul was in the sixth grade. Intellectually, Paul had a very high IQ. When he and I worked together, we held high-level conversations, and I was always impressed by what he had to say. Paul was also slow-moving, lethargic, and consistently had a mopey affect. He was not meeting the standards in many of his classes. As a trained special educator who believes that "kids do well if they can do well," I couldn't wait to start working with him. I pulled out every tool from my toolbox to help support him.

Honestly, I tried it all. We set up organizational systems together, ensured he completed his planner daily, communicated with his parents daily, used graphic organizers, had one-to-one meetings with his teachers, and the list goes on and on.

Nothing worked. Each day, Paul returned to school without his homework. During class, Paul sat there, glassy eyed and seemingly unwilling to do the work. Sometimes, he even laid his head down on his desk and fell asleep.

What I didn't know about at the time was Dr. Greene's Collaborative and Proactive Solutions (CPS) model and Plan B Approach:

> Collaborative & Proactive Solutions (CPS) is the evidence-based model of care that helps caregivers focus on identifying the problems causing concerning behaviors in kids and solving those problems collaboratively and proactively. The model is a departure from approaches emphasizing consequences to modify concerning behaviors.
>
> (Greene, 2010b)

This model encourages you to work collaboratively with the student to determine the lagging skill by using a discussion plan with the student called Plan B.

My mistake was that I was trying to solve this problem on my own without including Paul in the discussion.

Before I tell you the rest of Paul's story, allow me to explain more about Plan B (the discussion I should have had with him).

Plan B is a discussion between an adult (teacher, counselor, parent) and an individual exhibiting challenging behavior. The three steps plan is:

1 Empathy
2 Defining the Problem
3 Invitation

During the empathy stage, your role as the adult in this situation is to listen. You can start by saying something like, "I have observed that this (the problem) is happening. What's going on?"

Then listen and probe.

Plan B cheat sheet: learn more at https://livesinthebalance.org

---

Eventually, Paul failed his classes. I had multiple conversations with his teachers.

I said, "I truly don't believe any child is lazy. But maybe, just maybe, Paul is lazy?" I never felt good about it, but I just couldn't come up with any other reasons for his failure in school and my inability to reach him.

Paul moved at the end of the school year. In some respects, I felt thankful as I just couldn't seem to help him and that was crushing to me. Several months later, I received a message from Paul's mother. She explained that Paul had moved to a new school and was still struggling. She then filled me in on their home life. Earlier that spring, she discovered that her husband (Paul's dad) was an alcoholic. He drank all day and hid the bottles from his family. He was also emotionally and sometimes physically abusing Paul in the evenings.

No wonder Paul was glassy eyed and appeared mopey. No wonder he didn't do his work. He was experiencing severe trauma and none of us figured it out. In the end, I failed him. I changed my assumption that *kids do well if they can* to *kids do well if they want to* and let Paul down. It was easier that way.

With this attitude, I was able to say, "Well, I gave it all I could. Paul needed to do some of the work and he didn't. So, in the end, it was his fault."

Had I worked with this student and taken the CPS approach, perhaps we could have discovered what was happening in his home and worked together to get help and support for him and his family.

If only I could turn back time.

I still have educators and parents telling me that a child is lazy. Now, however, I no longer stay quiet. I hope you won't either. Come on and join me in shouting it from the rooftops: THERE'S NO SUCH THING AS A LAZY KID!

Key Takeaway: Be Empathetic

As the adage says, "When the only tool you have is a hammer, everything looks like a nail." I assumed I knew best and tried all my tools in Paul's case, but since my tools weren't working, I believed Paul was the issue.

Empathy is key. If you're having difficulties with a student, sit down with them and in a non-judgmental manner, help them identify the problem and come up with a possible solution together.

Reflection Questions

1 The concept of "children do well if they can" challenges the notion of laziness in children. How does this philosophy impact your understanding of a child's behavior? How might it change your approach when dealing with a child who is not meeting expectations?
2 Lori points out the importance of empathy in understanding a child's difficulties. How might applying more empathy in your practice affect your relationship with the children you work with? How might it affect the child's academic and personal development?
3 In Lori's story about Paul, the real issue was trauma at home. This highlights the importance of understanding a child's context. In what ways could you gather more information about a child's life outside of school or therapy sessions to better support them?

18 Navigating Relationships With the Most Important Member of Our Team
Fake It 'Til You Make It

Written by Lori

The following chapter is written from a teacher's perspective, focusing on building positive relationships with challenging students. Through a personal story, the author underscores the importance of empathy and effort in transforming student behavior. The intended audience includes educators and school professionals, offering insights to foster stronger student connections.

It's time for another "Lessons from Lori" story. After 25 years of teaching, it's okay to majorly mess up at times, but it never feels good. Never. However, I learn from each one and consider them opportunities to become a better educator.

In my fourth year of teaching, I worked at an international school in Saudi Arabia. I had a small class of 15 students who came from all over the world. They were a fun class. They got along well, collectively had a great sense of humor, and we just clicked – my dream class. I went home every day with a smile, charged up and ready to go the next day.

Around November of that year, I got word that a new student was coming. I was pleased as I knew this was the perfect group of kids to welcome in a new student. It's never easy for a teacher to prepare for a new student's arrival. We want our new student to feel welcome. We gather all necessary books, notebooks, organizational systems, pencils, and the like to have ready to go for that first day.

Austin (not his real name) arrived, and my classroom went from harmony to complete dissonance in a matter of minutes. Austin did everything he could to stand out. He was loud, constantly interrupted, was quite sneaky, and tried to make jokes to make his classmates laugh. Spoiler alert: the jokes were never funny. His behaviors caused some of my other students to misbehave, which was simply unacceptable to me.

I was crushed. My perfect classroom disintegrated before my eyes and I honestly didn't have the tools to fix it. I left school feeling exhausted each day and did not want to go back the following.

I vented to my colleagues in the lunchroom. They smiled and commiserated, but none had answers for me. Frustrated and defeated, I felt angry that the counselor placed this student into my perfect little class.

I tried giving him consequences for his behaviors. No change. I tried a behavior chart with rewards. No change. Nothing worked.

I didn't realize that all my feelings about Austin were obvious. The other students picked up on it and they got angry when he misbehaved. They began policing him. It all was just one negative experience for everyone.

I always enjoyed parent conferences. It gave me time to connect with families and share how great their children were. I loved showing their progress and success.

However, when Austin's mom came in, I certainly wasn't excited. Our exchange went something like this:

Me:	"Hi, Mrs. X. We are so happy Austin joined our classroom this year."
Mrs. X:	"Hmmm. Really?"
Me:	"What do you mean?"
Mrs. X:	"Austin doesn't think you like him."
Me:	"Well, I ..."
Mrs. X:	"You don't like my son."
Me:	"Of course, I like your son."
Mrs. X (now crying):	"Well, he doesn't think so, and I don't think so."
Me (now crying):	"I'm so sorry you both feel that way. I am going to fix this somehow."

That day was such a wakeup call. I loved teaching and was proud of the fact that I was a good teacher and the students enjoyed coming to school each day. I worked on building relationships with them all. Why hadn't I done that with Austin?

I thought to myself, "Austin thinks I don't like him. I'd better fake it 'til I make it. Even if I never do like him, he needs to think I do."

I took Austin aside the following week and said, "Austin, I'm sorry you don't think I like you. I want to change that feeling. Does that sound okay to you?" He nodded and smiled.

As the weeks went on, I learned about the dog he had to leave behind when he left his home country to move to Saudi Arabia. He loved his dog and missed him so much. I told him about leaving my cat, Carl, in the United States when I left and how I cried for months missing him. I learned that Austin loved baseball. I asked him to bring his mitt to school and we spent a few recesses throwing a softball back and forth to one another. Soon, the other kids in the class wanted to join in and we often played softball as a class together. Austin was a good artist and loved to doodle. I always liked to draw pictures to go with my lessons, so I had him come up to the board and draw some of them for me.

Soon, Austin's behaviors changed. He stopped interrupting and trying to tell jokes at every turn. Because of his cool doodles and our softball escapades, his classmates saw him as a great member of our classroom. And I learned that I adored Austin. What a great kid he was!

I learned so much from this experience. Building relationships with our students is the most important thing we can do as educators. Our kids must know that we care about them.

Relationship Side Story by Laurence Audet Beaupre

Laurence is a registered behavior technician (RBT) working and living in Singapore and is a native French Canadian. She has been providing in-home behavior therapy for individuals with developmental disabilities and is currently working on her master's degree and board certification in applied behavior analysis. The following is a true story and revelation about the importance of relationships when working with young children.

I started working with a girl about one year ago and at first, we developed a great bond. She was always happy to see me as I arrived for a session each day; however, after a few months, I saw some signs of deterioration in our relationship. For example, she often told her caregivers [that] she did not want to work with me and she started talking back to me in a very rude tone during our sessions. Then she started whining more and more during our sessions. All of these things began to decrease the speed of her learning acquisition. She even started to lose some of the skills that she had previously mastered. Despite these changes in behaviors, I continued to push her learning program forward and ignored the signs that our relationship needed work. I brought this to the attention of my supervisor, along with videos to support this. My supervisor was immediately able to see the issue and remind me to take a step back and look at the big picture.

Even though we place a lot of emphasis and importance on establishing a good relationship at the *beginning* of working with a child, I had long since forgotten this and began taking this crucial step for granted. My supervisor simply asked me to take a few steps back and analyze what I thought was interfering with my ability to be successful with her. I immediately saw the importance of RE-establishing a healthy/fun relationship. She recommended that I temporarily suspend all the program expectations and learning objectives to work on resetting our relationship, starting with pairing myself with fun and reinforcement.

Pairing occurs when the therapist tries to make themself fun to the child. I needed to rediscover what things she likes and dislikes. I just played with her and didn't place demands. The idea here is to make the child *want* to see me *want* to work with me and look forward to our time together. It was such a simple recommendation but so difficult to hear. It was evident that the relationship needed work, but I did nothing for so long, imagining that it would delay meeting our learning objectives. So, I swallowed my pride and started pairing again. It took about five sessions to get our relationship back to a place of trust and enjoyment. Re-establishing our healthy relationship was so valuable – it was the very thing we truly needed to get back to being able to work and learn together again. It was a valuable lesson to learn as a young therapist – it is the relationship that matters the most.

— (Laurence Audet Beaupre)

Our administrators facilitated the most beneficial meeting I've ever been to at my last international school as a teacher. After 25 years, that's saying a lot. They printed pictures of every student in the school with ample space below and sorted them by grade level. They placed all of these spaced out on tables. As a grade level, our task was to go around and write down something that we knew about each student. Once we finished our grade level, we could go to different grade levels and write about students we had previously known in a different capacity.

Some examples:

Dezi

- Loves popcorn (he eats it every day for a snack)
- Has two brothers
- Plays soccer
- Really funny
- Talented writer
- Has a dog named Lucy
- Moved here from Malaysia two years ago
- Has three best friends who do everything together

Samantha

- Is from Virginia, USA
- Has a cat named Shadow
- Loves the iPad
- Has two sisters
- Mom is a great baker
- Loves dinosaurs. Every story she writes is about them.

I enjoyed this activity because it gave us, as teachers, the ability to share what we knew about each student. It also allowed their current teachers to learn some things they may not have known about their students so they could start building a better relationship with them. I recommend all schools complete this exercise. If you cannot talk your administration into doing it schoolwide, try for your division or even your grade level. I guarantee that it is worth your time.

It's easy to say, "I love all my students."

Do you? It's okay if you don't. Really, it is. The important thing is that they don't know that. How can you fake it 'til you make it? Chances are if you build that relationship with your students, you will end up genuinely liking them. In the end, your heart will be happy and your students will feel respected, supported, and, yes, loved.

In conclusion, it's okay not to feel immediate warmth for every student we encounter. After all, we are humans first and educators or therapists second. The crucial aspect is to ensure our students never perceive this. We must always exude an attitude of care and respect, even when we have to "fake it 'til we make it." Because when we invest our time in understanding the nuances of our students' lives, in their joys, their fears, their aspirations, and their vulnerabilities, the tide invariably turns. We find ourselves drawn to their spirit and resilience, realizing that we've not only helped foster their growth but ours as well. Relationships are not mere tangential aspects of education or therapy; they are the very foundation. The transformative power of genuine connection can turn the most discordant classroom into a harmonious symphony and revive the dwindling flame of learning in a disheartened child. When all's said and done, it's not merely about liking our students, but about recognizing their uniqueness, appreciating their individuality, and nurturing their potential.

Reflection Questions

1 **Self-awareness and Emotional Management**: Reflect on a time when your personal feelings or biases may have affected your professional relationships, especially with students or clients. How did you address it, and what did you learn from the experience?
2 **Building Genuine Relationships**: Lori realized the importance of understanding and connecting with Austin beyond just academic expectations. Can you recall a similar experience where taking the time to know more about a student or client's personal life significantly changed your relationship or their outcomes? How did this experience shape your approach moving forward?
3 **Continuous Growth**: Laurence Audet Beaupre highlighted the significance of re-establishing a healthy/fun relationship when it starts to deteriorate. How do you ensure the consistent nurturing of your relationships with students or clients? What strategies or activities have you employed to rejuvenate a strained relationship?
4 **The Power of Collective Knowledge**: The schoolwide exercise of sharing insights about each student showed the importance of collaborative efforts in understanding students. How can schools, parents, and therapists further strengthen this collaboration to ensure a holistic understanding of a child's needs? How might this collective knowledge influence individualized strategies or interventions?

19 Navigating Miscommunication
Mind the Gap

Written by Lori

The next chapter is written from the perspective of a teacher who has experienced challenges in communication with parents. It provides insights and strategies for enhancing parent–teacher communication and is intended for teachers, educators, and school administrators who are looking to establish effective communication practices with parents. The focus on technology, work–life balance, and collaboration may also make it relevant to parents interested in understanding the dynamics of teacher communication.

When you ask a teacher what the most challenging part of their job is, they inevitably reply with one of two answers: "lack of school support" or "the parents." When you ask a special educator, they have the same issues as well as paperwork and emotional distress. With administration, there can be a multitude of reasons for difficulties, from leadership styles to a difference in philosophies. But when it comes to working with parents, the issue quite often revolves around misunderstanding and miscommunication.

We have all been there. We are having a great year reaching and teaching our students. Everything is going smoothly. We get along well and have built up a strong rapport with our students and they are learning. It feels great. And then, in that telltale ding alerting us to an incoming email, it all changes in an instant. We get the dreaded email from a parent with phrases that feel accusatory and, by all accounts, simply untrue:

"You're not challenging my child enough."

"You're not spending enough time with my child. She is entitled to 60 minutes of one-to-one instruction two times a week. Why aren't you teaching her like you should?"

"He already knows his alphabet. Why would you waste time working on that?"

"Stop taking her to that room where she gets to swing. She should be learning."

If you're like me in this type of situation, your immediate response is to defend yourself.

> Dear Mr. Halpert, Thanks for your email. I don't really understand why you think I don't spend my required time working with Layna. I work with Layna on Tuesdays and Thursdays for 60 minutes, as I told you during our last IEP meeting. In fact, I often extend our sessions as she needs so many breaks throughout instruction that she's actually getting closer to 70 minutes per session. Please let me know if you have any further questions or would like to discuss our schedule further.

Here is another example:

> Hi Penny, thank you for asking about the sensory room. As we've discussed multiple times, Caden uses the swing to regulate his sensory needs. This is not wasting his time with instruction. When his body is not regulated, he cannot learn, so trying to instruct him without meeting his sensory needs would not be beneficial. Please let me know if you'd like to learn more about this. Thank you.

Once I've finished fuming and have hit send on that email, I then vent to my colleague that these parents just don't get it. I work so hard with their children and all they do is write rude emails. What gives them the right?

Does this sound familiar? It's frustrating, isn't it?

Over 44% of teachers quit the profession within the first five years of teaching (Ingersoll, 2018). The reasons for this are many: lack of autonomy and support, parent overreach, student behavior, workload, and low wages, to name a few.

This chapter aims to try to mitigate just one of these factors, presumed parent overreach. Although I have experienced all of the previously cited reasons (and more) that made me feel like I wanted to quit at one time or another, it was in my relationships with parents that I felt I had the least amount of control. After many years of being both a parent and a teacher, I believe this can be broken down into one core issue: communication.

The most important thing in communication is hearing what isn't said.
—Peter Drucker

Communication

When I started teaching long, long ago, I communicated once per week with my students' families. I physically typed out a newsletter. Then, I would get some cute clipart (Suzy's Zoo was my favorite) or stickers, place them on the newsletter, and use the mimeograph machine to make enough copies for everyone in my class to take home on a Friday. By the way, if you have never had the opportunity to inhale the fumes from a ditto machine, then you are officially young! Interestingly, I had fewer complaints from families during these days. It's a simple fact. Parents didn't have communication tools at their fingertips. So, they couldn't simply email or text me with any thought or minor complaint or question they had.

Of course, technology advanced and so did the quality of my newsletters. So email came into play, and that's when things got considerably more difficult. Although I was still writing my weekly emails, I was getting more and more emails from parents. And if I didn't answer their question during the school day, I often got another email from them asking me why I hadn't responded.

"Because I'm teaching your child!" I wanted to shout.

It took several years, but I realized that this caused me to form a very unhealthy habit of checking my email throughout the school day. I was so afraid I would miss an email from my families that I put my email before my teaching. I would be in mid-lesson when I'd hear that *ding* that would shoot my dopamine levels through the roof. Inevitably I would then go through the "should I check it now or later" debate before ultimately checking. I finally hit bottom when I was teaching one day and the email notification went off. I looked at my students and one yelled, "You better check that, Mrs. Boll."

What was I teaching my students at that moment? I was teaching them that I placed more importance on whoever was emailing me than I did on them. I was teaching them that it was okay to drop everything you're doing and become distracted by whatever comes your way; that persisting through a difficult task was not important. And finally, what they were learning was not as important as what I saw on the screen.

That is not the type of teacher I wanted to be.

So, I drew the line and devised a new plan for communication broken into two categories: website and email.

Website:

- All curriculum information found on website
- All homework for the week on website
- Exemplars of work posted on website
- All learning outcomes for the week posted on website
- Supporting videos or documents posted on website

Email:

- Each Friday, a newsletter was sent out about what we did during the week, which included pictures, student feedback, and videos.

- Email responses: I only responded to emails in the morning before school and from 3:30–5:30 p.m. (These were the times that worked for me, but any teacher should feel empowered to set the times that work for them).
- If there were emergencies when the parent needed to contact me, they could call the office.
- No emails at the weekend!

This new policy had some hiccups along the way. Overall, this method created a healthy balance for me in my life and set the expectations for the families as well.

Having curricula and homework in one place, my student's parents didn't have to reach out to me with all of their questions anymore. I also added articles and resources so parents could understand the *whys* of certain types of work and therapy.

After I had the structure in place, I began to analyze why Mr. Halpert was upset about the schedule and why Penny didn't understand the benefits of her child using the sensory room. As a mom of a child with additional needs, I could completely empathize with them. They were upset because they couldn't see a complete picture of what was happening at school daily and when you can't see it yourself, you begin to fill in the gaps with what you believe is (or is not) happening.

That can be very scary. The families of students with additional learning needs have backgrounds and histories we are not always privy to knowing, so they can be filling in those gaps with misinformation based on prior history. We may not know that a parent struggled in school and was treated poorly by his teachers. We may not know that a family's child was sent to the office whenever she had difficulty self-regulating at a previous school.

As teachers, we need to assume our families want what is best for their child and help them understand that we have the same goal.

In other words, we need to fill in the gaps, so they don't have to.

The invention of Seesaw and other platforms helped bring communication up a notch to the point where all of the gaps are filled in. Seesaw serves as a communication system for families, a learning management system, and a portfolio for student work. I was able to effectively communicate with the families of my students who were nonverbal, as I could share all parts of their day.

For example:

- Henry Russo
- Eight years old
- 3rd Grade
- Autism
- Nonverbal

Henry's parents were apprehensive about his day. They said that he wandered around the room all day at his previous school and refused to participate. They did not believe he would learn to read or write. They said he had no friends.

With Seesaw, I was able to do the following:

1 Take a video of Henry following his visual schedule.
2 Take pictures of Henry using the reading program and narrate how the program worked.
3 Show pictures of Henry playing with friends in the sensory room and on the playground.
4 Take a video of Henry reading and writing.
5 Take a video of Henry participating in circle time.

By filling in the gaps for them through this incredible tool, Henry's parents soon understood how his day looked and they were able to see everything he was doing, so their fears and unease dissipated.

As the year went on, if his parents had questions, I would no longer take those questions personally. I listened and figured out how to show this loving family the answer.

Seesaw is fantastic for all students. I watched my general education colleagues use it in meaningful ways. Many of their students took ownership and created videos for their parents to share their learning.

My colleagues report that by using tools such as this, they receive fewer distressed emails from their families as well.

Parents ask questions because they care so much about their child and they are worried that they're the only ones who do. As teachers, we know we care as well. We can show our care by communicating well and often, so those doubts and worries turn to confidence and trust.

Misunderstandings can breed frustration, yet they also present an opportunity to foster clearer dialogue and enhance our collaborative efforts. Armed with empathy, respect, and the right communication tools, we can help alleviate the concerns of anxious parents, creating an environment of trust and mutual understanding. By fully acknowledging the issues that arise due to parental misconceptions and addressing these through mindful interaction and the power of platforms like Seesaw, we can bridge the communication gap. At the heart of this communication puzzle lies a shared goal: ensuring the best possible learning experience for our students. Every question, doubt, and interaction is an invitation to show just how much we care and how hard we are working toward this shared objective. By navigating miscommunication effectively, we can transform challenges into catalysts for building stronger, healthier relationships with parents, ultimately creating a more supportive and nurturing educational environment for our students.

Reflection Questions

1 **Self-Reflection on Communication**: Reflect on your own experiences in communicating with parents or teachers. Have you ever been on either side of a misunderstanding similar to the ones described in the chapter? How did it

make you feel, and what strategies did you use or could you have used to navigate the situation?
2. **Impact of Technology on Communication**: Considering the transition from traditional newsletters to online communication tools, do you believe technology has made it easier or more challenging for educators to communicate with parents? Why? What pros and cons can you identify from the chapter and your own experiences?
3. **Empathy and Assumptions**: Why do you think it's essential for teachers to operate from a place of empathy and avoid making assumptions about parents' backgrounds and intentions? How can educators be proactive in "filling the gaps" for parents to prevent miscommunication?
4. **Importance of Proactive Communication**: Drawing from the Seesaw example, how can proactive communication and visual evidence of a student's day-to-day activities alleviate parents' concerns? How can educators effectively use tools like Seesaw or other platforms to showcase their commitment to students and bridge communication gaps?

20 Navigating Team Success

Yes. We Can

Written by Lori

The following chapter is written from the perspective of an educator who emphasizes collaboration and teamwork among teachers, therapists, and parents. The chapter is intended for educational professionals, including teachers, speech-language pathologists, occupational therapists, and parents who are actively involved in the education and support of students. It offers insights into the importance of open communication and collaboration to achieve better outcomes for students, especially those with unique needs.

In the past several chapters, we've given you ideas and strategies on how educators and parents can work together, how educators and therapists can work with and build a strong rapport with students, and how parents and therapists can best communicate. Now we need to bring it all together and answer this question:

How can we all come together as educators, therapists, and parents to improve the quality of life for our students? No surprise here. We've shouted it from the rooftops multiple times in this book. The very best thing we can do as a team is to communicate!

If you're an educator, you might be thinking, "Yes, I communicate well with parents and my students. How do I communicate with the therapist?"

If you're a therapist, you might be thinking, "I communicate so well with parents and I'm a rockstar when it comes to building rapport with students. How can I communicate with my clients' teachers, so we are all working together on common goals?"

If you are a parent, you might be thinking, "I communicate with my child's teacher. I communicate with my child's therapists. However, it seems they don't communicate with each other."

It's tricky. There are so many scenarios that can impact a strong communication circle. Proximity to each other is one.

In my past school, I had the ideal situation. Our speech-language pathologist (SLP) and occupational therapist (OT) worked inside my classroom. Our team, which included the classroom assistants/paraprofessionals, met once per week to discuss our students and how we can better support them in achieving their IEP goals. If the students were exhibiting behaviors or challenges, we discussed those as well.

An example:

During one of our meetings, I mentioned that one of my nonverbal students, Dillon, was exhibiting behaviors during academic instruction. Once we sat down for our one-to-one instructional time, Dillon couldn't seem to remain seated. He stood up, jumped, made loud noises, and stimmed. His stim was flapping his arms up and down. While stimming is appropriate and accepted in the classroom, we knew that he stimmed to regulate his sensory system. We didn't understand why it needed regulating at this moment and why it only happened during one-to-one academic instruction.

Dillon was unable to discuss this with me. If he had a way to communicate how he was feeling, I would have involved him in the conversation using the technique mentioned earlier by Dr. Ross Greene. Our discussion went like this:

Me: During one-to-one instructional time, Dillon jumps up and down, vocalizes loudly, and stims. He only does this during this time which occurs three separate times during the school day, at 9:15 a.m., 10:30 a.m., and 1:00 p.m. (Note: I share facts to begin – no opinions or theories)

SLP: Could the work you're giving him be too difficult? Is he trying to communicate that it's too hard?

Me: I thought about that, so I tried giving him work that I know he can do independently. However, that didn't change anything.

Assistant: I work with Dillon one-to-one at 8:15 a.m. and he doesn't show any of these behaviors.

Me: Is it me? Could he feel like he doesn't want to work with me?

OT: Hmmm. That's a great question. Could he be reacting to a perfume you are wearing? Maybe he doesn't like how you smell.

Me: Okay, I won't take that personally. LOL. No, I don't think so. I don't wear perfume, and I haven't changed my shampoo or conditioner since last school year, and Dillon didn't do any of this last school year.

OT: Well, that's interesting.

Assistant: I wear perfume and he doesn't seem to react to mine.

OT: Okay, so he doesn't react to your perfume, Lori hasn't changed her shampoo or conditioner, so I'm under the impression that it's not related to smell. Where do you work with Dillon, Lori?

Me: Right here, at this table.

OT to Assistant: And where do you work with him?

Assistant: Over there. At that table.

OT: Let's sit in both places and take notice of our environment. Let's check out lights, sounds, etc.

SLP: Has anyone noticed that the air conditioning is blowing right on us at this table, where Lori works with Dillon?

Assistant:	Yes, that's why I refuse to work there. I can't stand that direct blast of air. Every time I do, I get really cold.
OT:	Could that be it?
Me:	Yes. It could be. Dillon's parents told us that he wears a hoodie sweatshirt in their house as he gets cold easily. Let me try working with Dillon tomorrow in this exact spot. However, I'm going to turn off the air conditioning before I work with him. Let's see how it goes.

The next day, I turned off the air conditioning before working with Dillon. What a change! Dillon sat down and worked. We had already worked out, as a team, that Dillon worked best when given choice. I laid out his three assignments each day and asked him which he wanted to do first. So that was important to know when working with him. On this day, we learned something new about Dillon. He was similar to the assistant and did not like cold air blasting at him. Once we turned that off, Dillon did all his work. He took some breaks to jump on a small trampoline we had, but he did all his work.

That conversation was vital. How long would it have taken me to work that out had I not worked with this team? Maybe I never would have, and what a shame that would have been for Dillon.

As a team, we also worked together when creating IEP goals. We knew each other's goals and would integrate our goals when working with our students.

One of the academic goals for our student, Dezi, was to learn his letters (sounds, names, and how to write them). So, our OT worked with Dezi to write his letters. However, she also incorporated sounds and letter names into her lessons. Our SLP worked on forming the sounds with Dezi's mouth structure and ensured that Dezi wrote the letters simultaneously. While teaching Dezi his letter sounds and names, I often worked on his core strength by having him support his body on a yoga ball. He bounced up and down while saying his letter names. Core strength was a goal from his OT. As he recited his letter names while bouncing, I focused on how he formed his letters with his mouth, which was part of his SLP goal. Working on our goals together helped us all focus on everything Dezi needed.

So yes, being in close proximity with the team is ideal. We all know, however, that not all groups are this lucky.

Many schools have a devoted SLP. Frequently, however, this one therapist might have more than 50 students on their caseload. The same is true for an OT. Another scenario is teletherapy. Many therapists now work with their clients online rather than in person. This is especially true in international schools as many do not have access to therapists, so parents hire these professionals online.

Can we expect educators and therapists to work as a team when faced with one of these scenarios?

Yes. We. Can. (Channeling my inner Bob the Builder here)

Not only can we expect it, but we should demand it of ourselves. Teachers should demand it. Therapists should demand it. Parents should demand it.

And when possible, students should demand it. We must work together to ensure our students are the most successful they can be.

So how can we do this if we are not in the same building, or in some cases, the same city, state, or country?

We utilize technology.

Zoom, Google Meets, and other platforms came to light during the pandemic and suddenly we all realized that we could have effective and collaborative meetings using these tools. Many therapists build documentation and meeting time into their therapy sessions, so devoting time each week to these discussions is preferred and expected.

Technology enables us to communicate with one another both asynchronously and synchronously. Therefore, it is highly possible to work collaboratively and ensure we are all on the same page and making informed program decisions when supporting our students. So, while being in close proximity is ideal, it is not a requirement and cannot be used as an excuse for lack of communication.

While we prefer apps or programs where we can track goals and behaviors, in the end it doesn't matter which program we use. What matters is that we are communicating, collaborating, and learning together as a team. What matters is that we listen, take action, and make informed decisions together. What matters is that we don't work as silos but instead as synergetic partners.

What matters is our students.

In conclusion, open communication between educators, therapists, and parents is crucial. We have shared real-life scenarios, valuable tools, and technology and provided insights into the potential barriers that might exist. Regardless of the roles we play or the scenarios we find ourselves in, we are bound by a common goal – to improve the quality of our students' lives. It's not about the perfect setting or the proximity to each other. It's about bridging the gaps, learning to listen, making informed decisions, and most importantly, fostering a synergetic partnership focused on the students' needs. This collaborative approach, we firmly believe, is the driving force that ensures our collective efficacy. So, while "Yes. We. Can" may seem like a simple slogan, it indeed embodies our collective strength and determination. Together, we can navigate the path to success, and in doing so, shape a brighter future for our students.

Reflection Questions

1 **Collaboration in Focus**: Given the real-life scenario with Dillon, how does this narrative emphasize the importance of educators, therapists, and parents collaborating for the well-being of a student?
2 **Communication Barriers and Solutions**: The chapter highlights different challenges that may arise when trying to maintain a communication circle between educators, therapists, and parents. Reflect on a time when you faced a communication barrier in your professional or personal life. How did you overcome it, and how can those strategies be applied in the context of ensuring student success?

3 **Technological Assistance**: With the rise of teletherapy and digital tools aiding communication, how do you think the landscape of student-therapist-teacher collaboration will change in the next decade?
4 **The Core of Collaboration**: The chapter concludes with a strong emphasis on the student being at the center of all efforts. How can educators, therapists, and parents ensure they are always keeping the student's needs at the forefront of their collaboration, especially when faced with differing opinions or approaches to challenges?

In our first two sections, we took you on the journey of Discovering and Navigating special learning needs through the perspectives of parents, educators, and therapists in the field. By sharing these points of view, we hope to help create authentic Collective Efficacy, realizing that this is what enables all parties to be all they can be. As Donohoo et al. remind us, "success lies in the critical nature of collaboration and the strength of believing that together [parents, students, therapists, and teachers] can accomplish great things. This is the power of Collective Efficacy."

We recognized that improving rapport with one another dramatically affects our ability to be as helpful as possible in our efforts with our students. Further, if we overlook this covariate, it's likely to serve as a barrier to success.

This third and final section focuses on Empowering the members of our Collective Efficacy team. We identified self-care as another potential barrier to being the best that we can be as members of the support team. It's likely that you already have some understanding of the concept of self-care, as it has received a considerable amount of attention in popular media around the world. It is often overlooked in the literature and needs additional research.

This section elaborates on the variables that interfere with our ability to take the best care of our physical and mental health. We also make a case as to WHY this additional covariate is essential – not just in serving our students – but in life at large.

Part III
Empowering

21 Empowering You to Have a Difficult Conversation
Turn In

Written by Lori

In the next chapter, Lori turned to experts in conflict resolution and communication techniques in the field of special education. The chapter is intended to better equip educators, administrators, and other professionals in special education, as well as parents and guardians of students with special needs for these inevitable conversations. The chapter offers insights and practical strategies for effectively navigating challenging conversations and fostering collaborative relationships.

If you're like me, you avoid conflict at all possible costs. However, when you are in the field of special education as a parent, teacher, or therapist, conflicts are bound to arise. So how should we deal with them?

If you're like me, you would prefer to hide in a corner, plug your ears, and sing "la la la la la" at the top of your lungs so you can block out that conflict noise. This, of course, is not a great strategy and one I do not recommend. It's also not healthy for any of the parties. In any relationship, conflict is expected.

It took years for me to be able to have a difficult conversation and honestly, I'm still practicing this skill.

Amanda and I both believe the best path toward managing conflict is to be proactive and that we should set our interactions up to be successful. So, we turned to the research by relationship experts Drs. Jon and Julie Gottman. Relationship experts? Say what? Yes. These researchers focus on romantic relationships; however, they developed a method for proactively managing conflict and having difficult conversations that apply to all relationships, not just the romantic kind.

In a seminar Dr. Jon Goodman gave in 2011, (*John Gottman: How to build trust – YouTube* 2011), he mentioned first that the essential pillar of any relationship is trust. To build trust, he suggests using the acronym that his graduate student, Daniel Shimoto, created: ATTUNE. See Figure 21.1.

The A in ATTUNE stands for awareness. ATTUNE basically means that we're aware that another party in our collaborative team has an emotion. Little hints of this might be short, to the point emails with no greeting; someone quickly walking by you in a hallway without acknowledging you; or facial expressions sharing their emotions. When you recognize that someone is having an emotion, you have a choice; "turn in or turn out."

140 *Empowering*

> **A**wareness
> **T**urning Toward
> **T**olerance
> **U**nderstanding
> **N**on-defensive responding
> **E**mpathy

Figure 21.1 ATTUNE

That brings us to T: Turn in. Gottman explains that when you "turn into" the person, you acknowledge they're feeling a certain way. Turning in demonstrates you care, even if it sometimes means putting their needs ahead of yours at that moment. Sure, it might be easier to say, "Ugh, I don't want to take Mrs. Jasper's phone call right now, as I really need to make these copies." However, you let Mrs. Jasper know that she is important and that what she says matters to you by taking the phone call. According to Gottman, "When you choose to turn away, trust erodes in the relationship." (*John Gottman: How to build trust – YouTube* 2011).

The second T stands for tolerance. As hard as it is, we must recognize that there may be two (or more) different emotions or viewpoints. Once we practice tolerance, we can move toward the U in ATTUNE, which means understanding other people's emotions. This is where empathy and compassion come in. We ask ourselves, "Why is this person feeling this way?" and explore. Was there a miscommunication? Are they confused (usually due to a miscommunication), or is there something happening on a deeper level that we may not be able to figure out at the time? While all these steps to building trust are essential, tolerating and understanding other viewpoints are vital.

We'll move on to the letters N and E in ATTUNE after this short story.

I'd like to share an experience that helps demonstrate the importance of building relationships between families and teachers. During the middle of one school year, I received notice that I was getting a new student in my learning support classroom. This news always filled me with both excitement and trepidation.

"Oh, I hope my new student fits in well with the others."

"I'm so excited for this new energy."

"I hope this student has a nice parent."

"I really hope this student adjusts well."

And so on …

Upon reading through my new student's file, I learned some things about him. The previous school described the student as a kind young man with a specific learning disability in reading. Further, he worked hard and described him as showing difficulty with emotional regulation demonstrated by behavior data taken by his previous school.

"Easy enough. He'll fit right in," I thought. I read further and that's when I realized that I knew this student, and he came with a reputation. His reputation was not based on him but on his mother. His mother was known as the one who yelled at everyone on the team no matter how well a meeting was going. My excitement about getting a new student quickly dissipated and I began experiencing anxiety about his arrival instead.

I prepared for his arrival by sending out a welcome email and asking for his parents to fill in some information for me. I never received a response, so that was frustrating. I also heard from the principal that the parent was frustrated by that email I sent as she believed I was trying to "butter her up." I was livid. I sent that same email out to all of my families in the past and no one ever complained. Most were happy that I was trying to get to know their children. I found myself perseverating on the arrival of this student and how upset I was that she called the principal to complain about me. Thoughts of, "This will be a miserable experience. This mother is the worst. I can't wait till this year is over," filled my head and played itself repeatedly in a loop.

The student arrived with his mother on his first day. The woman had a scowl on her face and I immediately felt the need to be defensive. But something stopped me and instead, I smiled. Trust me when I tell you that this was not easy for me. If I think someone doesn't like me, it upsets me greatly and I immediately go on the defensive. At any rate, I welcomed her and her son to the classroom and showed them around. I explained how the classroom schedule and my support plan. She eventually left and her son had a great first day of school. Phew.

The next day she returned. Uh oh. She spent 10 minutes speaking to me about her worries about her son. I remember thinking, "Ugh, I really don't have the time for this. I really need to finish preparing for my day." But I listened and tried to give her some reassurance.

The next day, she arrived again and took another ten minutes of my time. The next day it happened again, and so on and so on. I vented with a colleague who said, "You need to stop this now, Lori. Tell this woman that while you enjoy talking to her, you need to spend your morning time getting things ready for *all* your students."

I was ready to do just that the following day (after practicing at home what I was going to say in the mirror) when something again stopped me. Instead, I met the mother at the door and chatted with her. I made a joke of some sort and she laughed. By the end of the first three weeks, I realized that by not stopping these meetings at the beginning, I had created a "habit," and that habit was not going to end.

And I was okay with that. The reason? I could see that this mother started to trust me by having these daily discussions. So, I adjusted my routine instead. It turns out that I didn't need those 10 minutes each day and that building this relationship trumped prep time. As a bonus, our speech therapist also started taking advantage of this time to come and join us in our conversations. Eventually, we learned about each other's families and more about our backgrounds. After many months, I realized that this mother had a difficult upbringing and had a deep hatred of school systems. She was labeled "stupid" by her parents and teachers and felt she never had a chance. She didn't want the same for her son.

We interrupt this story to go back to the ATTUNE acronym. At this point, you probably recognized that my team and I had already, without knowing it at the time, used the first four letters of the acronym. We were aware of emotions and turned into them rather than turning away. Through our discussions, we began to see that she had reasons behind her frustrations. Reserving those 10 minutes at the beginning of each school day was just what this mom needed from us to earn her trust. That trust built the foundation of our future relationship.

The next letter of the acronym, N, stands for responding nondefensively. At our first IEP meeting, the team was nervous. This mother was known for her outbursts, and although we had built up trust with her, and we all quite frankly liked her a lot, her reputation was well known in the district. We started our meeting in our usual manner, asking for all the positives we had seen in her son since joining the school. He was part of this conversation as well, so he shared how he made some friends and was starting to learn about vowel pairs, one of his targeted IEP objectives, among other things. While we shared these positives, one of us listed them down on a poster, so they remained visible throughout the meeting. His mother beamed with pride throughout this discussion.

Soon we jumped into challenges and his goals and objectives. The meeting was going well and the rest of the team and I were giving each other invisible high fives when suddenly the mother remarked, "You don't challenge him enough. This school doesn't do enough for him!"

I was floored. What did she mean? She had never mentioned this before. How dare she? At this point, I looked down, took a deep breath, and said, "Thank you for sharing this with all of us. Please help us understand why you feel this way." Again, this sort of thing was never my strength. However, I also knew that in the past, when I responded defensively, it never ended well. That one deep breath helped me slow down, pause, and rethink how I wanted to respond. Once she realized we were ready to listen, her voice regulated and she explained that his homework seemed too easy and she was afraid we were "dumbing it down for him. I told you I don't want him having the same experience as me in school."

Ahhh. That made so much sense. Of course, she was feeling this way. She had a bad experience and her greatest fear was for her son to experience the same thing. We responded with empathy (the last letter in the acronym). We explained that homework, by design, was made for him to practice what he already knew and intended to be done independently, without any support. We showed her more of what he was learning in the classroom and the manner in which he was learning the core curriculum. You could see the relief on her face once she understood this. My biggest regret was that I didn't explain this to her beforehand so she wouldn't have felt that fear for so long.

The meeting ended and we were all stunned when, as this mother was leaving, she gave us a big hug and thanked us. She also asked for the poster we made of her son's strengths so she could hang it in his room to remind him of his strength.

We learned from that experience. I learned to communicate more about the curriculum with families to help reassure them. I also learned that responding nondefensively was another key to successful collaboration. When she had issues she wanted to discuss with us, she did so calmly. Sure, occasionally, she raised her voice. However, we had built up that foundation of trust by that time, so we knew that her anger was more about the situation than about us, so we stopped being defensive and listened to her while seeking to understand her point of view. In the end, we were a true team, and our number one goal was to do right by her son. She felt it and we felt it. Most importantly, her son felt it.

When You Need to Have a Difficult Conversation

While we wish it to be so, sometimes it's not all sunshine and roses.

Conflicts happen, and having conflict within the team does not mean the team is weak or dysfunctional. It's how we deal with that conflict that strengthens or strains our team. Whether we are a parent, a therapist, or a teacher, bringing up a difficult topic can be stress inducing. And, if you're on the other side of receiving the strongly worded email, it can cause high anxiety.

Let's say you've tried to build the foundation of trust and it's just not there yet. Or, even if the trust is there, having a protocol for managing conflict is helpful. How then do you deal with disputes that arise?

Using Hattie's research on Collective Efficacy, effective teams practiced turn taking and empathic listening while meeting. They also started all meetings with an agenda restating the goal. The research also showed that having a leader who ensured all of this took place usually meant the team had a much better chance of success.

Another key part of the research states that we must presume competence and have high expectations for each other and the student at the heart of the discussion.

We suggest the following protocol for when you need to have a difficult conversation.

1 Request a meeting
2 Share the topic of the meeting
3 Create an agenda for the meeting
4 During the meeting:

    a Follow the agenda
    b Introduce the problem using an "I" message
    c Listen to understand vs. Listening to respond
    d Set an action
    e Arrange a follow-up meeting

Request a Meeting and Use I Messages

Keep in mind that whether you are a student, parent, teacher, or therapist, you have the right to call a meeting at any time. Individualized Educational Plan (IEP) meetings are generally held once per year, but there is no rule stating you cannot meet at other times.

We recommend meeting whenever there is a conflict, as this brings the issue to the forefront, enabling you to prevent it from growing into something bigger. If you have a problem arise, first and foremost, do not keep it to yourself. All this serves to do is create a deep feeling of resentment. Before you know it, a small problem has blossomed into a big one. Please be sure to call or send a polite email to the person with whom you would like to meet. No one wants to be pulled aside in a school hallway to be told of a problem.

Share the Topic of the Meeting

Teachers, we've all been there. It's Friday afternoon and you get a phone call from the school secretary, "The principal would like to see you first thing Monday morning."

"Oh, can you tell me what it's about?"

"No, she will see you on Monday."

So, what happens all weekend long? Well, if you're like me, you fret and ask yourself, "What did I do wrong?" You run through 10,000 scenarios in your head and make yourself sick with worry. By the time Monday rolls around, you're a mess and most likely are not in the best frame of mind to teach young minds.

Parents, have you ever received an email from a teacher requesting a meeting with no topic? Ugh. It's the worst.

So, request a meeting with a topic.

Dear Mr. K,

I'd appreciate it if we could meet sometime soon to discuss Susan's math homework. At her last school, she was already adding numbers to 10. I wonder why she isn't showing you that she can do this skill at school and would like to learn more about the math program.

Thank you,

This type of communication tells the teacher exactly what the parent wishes to discuss and gives them time to prepare for the meeting. When teachers are surprised at a meeting's topic, they cannot gather the materials and items they may need to help clear up the issue.

Dear Mr. & Mrs. Rodriguez,

I'm looking forward to meeting with you and the rest of Salito's team this Wednesday. As we have discussed, his hitting others has increased this week to four times. We wonder if you can give us any insight into what might be happening during recess time to cause him to become emotionally dysregulated. We hope to work together to develop a plan to support Salito.

Sincerely,

In this scenario, the teacher reached out to the parents to help them devise a plan that might help support Salito and his emotional regulation challenges. No blame was placed and it calls for a team approach. As we mentioned at the beginning of this book, Hattie's research on Collective Efficacy showed that effective teams practiced turn taking and empathic listening while meeting. These teams also started all meetings with an agenda that restated the goal. Hattie's research showed the importance of assigning a facilitator who ensured it all took place. Teams who accomplished this had a much better chance of achieving a favorable outcome in terms of Collective Efficacy.

Create an Agenda for the Meeting and Send It Ahead of Time

Creating an agenda to follow during a meeting ensures that everyone's voice is heard, there is a clear path to follow, and the next steps are taken. Disseminating it before the meeting enables each team member to prepare.

During the Meeting

During the meeting, make sure to follow the agenda. Assign a facilitator to ensure that each person is heard and feels heard.

Ensure that each person in the meeting uses "I" messages. This helps everyone as by using an I message, you are sharing how you are feeling rather than blaming anyone. For example, "I'm concerned that Angela is not getting all of her speech-language therapy meetings each week" sounds like a valid concern. "You're not working with Angela enough" sounds like a direct attack.

Once the meeting begins, it is vital to listen for understanding vs. listening to respond. Research shows that only 10% of the population are active, empathic listeners. Active listening involves focusing on the speaker, avoiding all distractions (squirrel!), and focusing on the topic. Listen to what the person says. Aim to understand and empathize with their point of view. We may not always see it from their angle, but if we try, they will know, which means so much. In the end, it is not a matter of being right. It is about being understood. Rather than replying immediately after the person finishes, ask a clarifying question. Show them that you hear their concern and would like more information. During this portion of the meeting, never interrupt the speaker as this immediately kills trust, and they'll often leave the meeting thinking, "Well, they already had their mind made up. They wouldn't even listen to me." Once you have asked the clarifying question, share your thoughts on the topic. Hopefully, you've cleared up any misunderstanding that may have occurred. If not, at the very least, you have continued to build that foundation of trust.

Once everyone has been heard, set an action. If the conflict is not resolved, the action item might simply be to set up a new meeting to discuss it further. However, most of the time, you should be able to come up with an action plan. Schedule a follow-up meeting even if you believe you've "solved the issue" at the meeting.

> *Ex. Now that we know Salito is coming home and sharing that Henri keeps cutting in front of him in line, we can work on a few things. 1) We'll work with Henri and help him understand that cutting is not okay, and 2) We'll work with Salito to have him come and talk with an adult if Henri cuts rather than hitting Henri. Let's have a follow-up meeting in one week to see how this is going for everyone.*

We've mentioned it before and it bears repeating that Hattie's research states that we must presume competence in each other and have high expectations for each other and the student at the heart of the discussion. If we can remember this throughout any conflict, we will be better for it in the end.

We hope we've given you some tools to go out there and have a difficult conversation. Please don't be like me and avoid them at all possible costs. Trust me when I say: I learned the hard way and a hard conversation is better than no conversation. Sometimes you just have to pull those fingers out of your ears and embrace the "conflict noise." Now you have some strategies and data to do so.

Reflection Questions

1. **Self-awareness and ATTUNE**: Reflecting on your past experiences in conflicts, can you identify moments where you might have benefited from the ATTUNE approach? How might you have handled a situation differently by being more aware of another person's emotion or turning into them instead of away?
2. **Building Trust Through Consistent Communication**: Think about the story of the teacher and the mother who initially seemed confrontational. Why do you believe their daily interactions played such a pivotal role in establishing trust? How might this inspire you to engage in more consistent communication with those you work with, even if it's challenging at first?
3. **Response to Feedback**: In the IEP meeting scenario, the teacher took a moment to pause and respond nondefensively to the mother's concern. How do you typically react to criticism or feedback, especially when it catches you off-guard? What strategies can you employ to ensure you listen empathetically and respond nondefensively?
4. **Managing Difficult Conversations**: Based on the suggested protocol for handling difficult conversations, think about a time you had to engage in a challenging dialogue. How might following this protocol have changed the outcome or process of that conversation? Moving forward, how can you implement this protocol in both professional and personal settings?

22 Empowering Confidence
Imposter Syndrome

Written by Dr. Ly

The next chapter is written from the perspective of someone knowledgeable in mental health and with a personal understanding of the challenges of imposter syndrome. It is intended for individuals who may be experiencing these feelings in various aspects of their lives, such as career, academics, or personal relationships. By detailing the prevalence of the issue, its negative effects, and providing specific strategies to overcome it, the chapter aims to guide and empower those struggling with imposter syndrome to acknowledge and work through these feelings for personal growth and overall well-being.

A recent study was published indicating that up to 82% of people face feelings of "imposter phenomenon," struggling with the sense they are a fraud (Bravata et al., 2020. This sense of fraud spans all disciplines and across genders. Many of you will be nodding your head and perhaps this number doesn't surprise you; many others will be wondering what imposter syndrome is.

An article published in June 2021 in American Psychological Association's magazine *Monitor on Psychology* indicated that these feelings of being a fraud might contribute to anxiety and depression, less risk taking in careers, and even career burnout (Palmer, 2021). Clinical psychologist Audrey Ervin, PhD, adds, "there's an ongoing fear that high-achieving individuals usually experience that they're going to be 'found out' or unmasked as incompetent or unable to replicate past successes." These psychological ramifications are a huge problem both on the macro level in stifling career growth and progress but more on the personal level, making people feel inadequate and increasing burnout.

What a burden for 82% of the population to be carrying around with us all the time. Can you imagine how that one element influences nearly every one of our interactions with our colleagues and clients? Imagine what we could do if we could overcome this. Imagine if we were secure and did NOT feel like a fraud. Knowing just how many of us (myself included) suffer from these feelings at some point, it seems crucial to unveil and address them head-on.

For a more in-depth look at imposter syndrome, you may want to read *Own Your Greatness: Overcome Imposter Syndrome, Beat Self-Doubt, and Succeed in Life* by Lisa Orbe-Austin and Richard Orbe-Austin, which offers a slew of helpful advice and sheds insight on this modern-day social problem (2020).

The article in *Monitor on Psychology* went on to give seven strategies to help overcome imposter feelings:

1 **Learn the facts** – Address cognitive distortion contributing to the feelings of fraud.
2 **Share your feelings**. Sharing with others fosters connection, reduces loneliness, and curbs imposter feelings.
3 **Celebrate your successes**. Learning to internalize our success reduces self-doubt.
4 **Let go of perfectionism**. Adjust your standards for success. Resist the urge to view unmet standards as failures and instead reframe them as learning opportunities.
5 **Cultivate self-compassion**. Shift from an external focus of self-worth to an internal one. Learn to be okay as you are, without your accomplishments.
6 **Share your failures**. Discussing failures with others allows people to identify with you and leads to connection rather than disconnection.
7 **Accept it**. Accepting these feelings is natural and expected, allowing them not to grow bigger than they are.

What to Do About It

Learn the Facts

We all have cognitive distortions on occasion; however, some of us get stuck into habitually distorting our thoughts. According to Psych Central, cognitive distortions are exaggerated patterns of thinking not based on facts. It leads you to view things more negatively than they are (2022). Debbie Hampton (2016) writes a lot about the ways our brains influence our mental health in her work on *The Best Brain Possible* (https://thebestbrainpossible.com/), stating that "if you want to change the way you feel, you've got to change the way you think."

Often, we feel a certain way from the stories we tell ourselves. Sometimes we presume we know what others are thinking, but you may discover you were wrong if you ask them. High-achieving individuals are often their own worst critics. Even if you are compassionate and understanding toward others, you can be harsh on yourself and assume that you know what others are thinking. A surefire way to debunk those mistaken beliefs or cognitive distortions is to ask people directly what they are thinking.

High-achieving individuals are often their own worst critics. Even if you are compassionate and understanding toward others ...

An exercise my therapist had me do early at the start of my therapy was to write down what I *thought* others were thinking and then *ask* them directly what they were thinking and see how the two compared. It is powerful to realize that you are wrong in assuming others think the worst about you, but they often believe almost the opposite! I'll bet you a nickel that if you believe something critical about yourself and the way others perceive you after you ask, you'll find that you are wrong about these assumptions in most cases. You won't know until you challenge faulty thinking.

Cognitive Behavior Therapy is excellent for combating negative self-talk, cognitive distortions, and other faulty thinking. A key component to counter these tricks our brains play on us is engaging in positive, supportive statements. In *The Anxiety & Phobia Workbook – 6th Edition* Edmund J. Bourne (2015) claims that there are three basic types of distortions:

1 Overestimating a Negative Outcome
2 Catastrophizing
3 Underestimating Your Ability to Cope

If you change the way you THINK, you change the way you FEEL.

Let us look at each of these a bit more closely. First, **Overestimating a Negative Outcome** means that we mistakenly overestimate the odds of something terrible happening. Most of the distortion and worry stems from "what-if statements." "What if the plane falls out of the sky and I die?" "What if I fail this exam and flunk out of graduate school." To refute overestimating a negative outcome, you should ask yourself – "When I view this objectively, what are the odds of the negative outcome happening?"

Next, **Catastrophizing** is a distorted thought where you think, "if a negative outcome did occur, it would be catastrophic, overwhelming, and unmanageable." Catastrophic thoughts usually contain statements like, "I couldn't handle _____," "I'd be completely overwhelmed if _____ happened," or "my friend will never forgive me if I do _____." To refute catastrophizing, you must ask yourself, "IF the worst case did happen, is it true that I wouldn't be able to handle it?" Try to see into the future and extrapolate that IF the worst case did happen, then what? Typically, when terrible things happen, most people switch into survival mode and manage the situation at the moment. After the emergency subsides, when people handle their emotions, the key point is that people primarily do MANAGE when bad things happen.

The third distorted way of thinking is **Underestimating Your Ability to Cope**. When one engages in this distortion, you don't recognize your ability to cope when bad things happen. Bourne noted that typically when you underestimate your ability to cope is usually implicit in your catastrophic thinking. Given this, how you refute underestimating your ability to manage usually occurs by answering catastrophic thinking with a more objective appraisal. For example, "In the unlikely event that I trip and fall when giving a presentation, I would dust myself off and get up. I am perfectly capable of handling the situation and can even laugh at the absurdity."

Share Your Feelings

If you don't trust your own "facts," perhaps enlist other people. Sharing your feelings about being an imposter can reduce loneliness and open doors for others to share what they see in you, which can curb imposter feelings. However, be strategic with whom you share. Only share with people you trust and with whom you have mutual respect.

Sometimes simply naming your uncomfortable feelings aloud is enough to squelch them. Being honest and transparent about what you feel can often relieve you from feeling them more fully. I find that calmly stating aloud, "I'm feeling nervous" or "I am feeling anxious about …" or "I'm feeling like I am unsure what to do, but I don't want to seem unprepared" helps. Additionally, naming feelings aloud invites others to connect with you and that same feeling in someone else. There is evidence that sharing our emotions, especially the vulnerable ones (i.e., shame, embarrassment, grief), actually sets the stage for meaningful connection with others (Brown, 2021).

Sharing feelings with others models a good emotional regulation strategy for those around us: kids, peers, and family members. Next time you feel strong emotions, especially if they relate to feelings of fraud, try simply stating your feeling aloud. You may be surprised by the result. It seems super simple but can be an effective technique.

> *"... sharing our emotions, especially the vulnerable ones (i.e., shame, embarrassment, grief), actually sets the stage for meaningful connection with others."*
> —*Brene Brown*

Celebrate Your Successes

People with imposter feelings tend to dismiss their accomplishments, exacerbating the experience. Sometimes in the busyness of our daily lives, we forget to take time to acknowledge ourselves and what we do well. I know that I tend to grind, accomplish, move on, and don't take time to enjoy or celebrate. We need to work on celebrating to get fully comfortable in ourselves and feel empowered. A book published by Drs. Orbé-Austin's entitled *Own Your Greatness: Overcome Imposter Syndrome, Beat Self-Doubt, and Succeed in Life*, is recommended for further reading, especially if this is difficult for you. In *Own Your Greatness*, they posit that you can alleviate self-doubt and learn to internalize your success by celebrating your accomplishments.

Small things do add up. When I was living overseas in China, we noticed after five years that we weren't celebrating American holidays – because we didn't get the days off from work. We were also not celebrating Chinese holidays, which we did have off from work, but weren't meaningful to us. We realized we weren't celebrating anything at the end of five years. The next time we went overseas, we made a pact that we would celebrate the holidays that were important to us, including our successes.

Given that many of us with imposter feelings tend to hyper-focus on the negative things, it is no surprise that we overlook our successes and accomplishments. If we don't take the time to pause and celebrate, life will pass us by. Life can be complicated and overwhelming, but it is far more complex and unpleasant if we don't stop and smell the roses. Stop and take stock of the good stuff.

Let Go of Perfectionism

Letting go of perfectionism is not about lowering the bar but adjusting your standards for success. When you allow yourself to adapt, you resist the urge to see anything less than perfect as failures and instead reframe them as opportunities to learn and grow.

There is a lot to say about perfectionism, but the most significant point I want to drive home here is that THERE IS NO SUCH THING AS PERFECTION – not in life and not in people. Now, look in the mirror and repeat that sentence until you fully understand there is no such thing. Thinking that you (and others around you) can or need to be perfect is the source of mental suffering and conflict between people.

This strategy cannot be overstated – LET. GO. OF. PERFECTIONISM! Sorry for all caps and exclamation points, but this is a critical point for perfectionists. I've had so many mixed feelings about perfectionism throughout my life. As I enter my 40s, it is crystal clear that perfectionism is a trap and is often masked or disguised as something good. It will save you a lot of heartache and trouble if you can find a way to see through perfectionism and its trickery. Let it go and you won't be disappointed. I've been aware of perfectionism as a false prophet for about eight years (yes, it took me 32 years to realize this), yet it still creeps up on me. Much like sleeping, it's never done or complete. For it to be helpful, you must do it regularly.

Perfectionism has been at the root of nearly every one of my emotional struggles. What I do know is that when I can see perfectionism for what it is – a trap – I can get past it more quickly and label it not as something to be strived for but as faulty thinking. Join me in calling it what it is and stop this culture of striving for perfection. It doesn't exist, and it causes a lot of people to feel like a failure for not being able to attain the unattainable. Let's help save ourselves from causing more feelings of inadequacy and help those around us, especially the next generation, see through this faulty thinking.

Cultivate Self-Compassion

To begin the journey of cultivating self-compassion, Ervin suggests using mindfulness to shift from an external focus of self-worth to an internal one. This shift in focus can allow you to let go of perfectionism and learn to recognize the feelings of fear of being an imposter. To cultivate self-compassion, you will need to learn to be okay as you are, without any "accomplishments."

To cultivate self-compassion, you will need to learn to be okay as you are, without any "accomplishments."

Caring for those we love comes naturally for many of us – our children, grandchildren, husbands/wives, brothers/sisters, and parents. We are kind, considerate, and compassionate. If one of them makes a mistake, we help pick them back up and build them up. We dismiss errors or mistakes and celebrate accomplishments. Yet, when we make a mistake ourselves, we are harsh, judgmental, and critical in a way that we would never dream of being with someone we love. This stern internal critic is constantly playing in the back of our minds. When we achieve, we brush it off and move on to achieve MORE. When we make mistakes, we call ourselves names or, for some, even berate ourselves. Not cultivating self-compassion has become a habit developed throughout a lifetime and sometimes we aren't even aware of the internal dialogue.

Not cultivating self-compassion has become a [bad] habit developed throughout our lifetime.

My therapist helped me see my lack of compassion for myself by asking what my young daughter or even my beloved pet dog, Bon Bon, needed to do to be lovable. That's easy – nothing! There's nothing they need to say, do, or be in order to be lovable. Why should this be any different for me/us?

Another great exercise my therapist had me do early on was verbalizing what I was going through. I explained my struggles and pointed blame in a hypercritical way (at myself). After I finished, she asked me to describe the same circumstances, but as if my daughter was the one going through the struggles. Gosh, what a difference when I told about myself as the epicenter of the struggle versus my precious 3-year-old. I was soft and kind and compassionate. Like I would for anyone else I love who is going through a hard time. Why is it that we can't extend the same kindness or self-compassion to ourselves? I can't explain why this is, only that it is vital how we treat ourselves. If we want to learn how to be *better* for those we love, we must not overlook being kind and compassionate first and foremost to ourselves. Treat being kind to yourself as if it were as important as being kind to others. Fostering self-compassion will forever change how you occur in the world. For future reading on perfectionism, I highly encourage you to read Brené Brown's book *The Gifts of Imperfection: Let Go of Who You Think You're Supposed to Be and Embrace Who You Are* (2010).

> *If we want to learn how to be better for those we love, we must not overlook being kind and compassionate first and foremost to ourselves.*

To help you work through your perfectionism, I recommend working your way (ideally with the help of a therapist) through an anxiety workbook (perfectionism and anxiety are inextricably linked). There are several good workbooks on the market. The one I've used most recently is *The Anxiety & Phobia Workbook – Seventh Edition*, published in 2020. You'd be amazed at how much insight you gain just by writing things in a personalized way in a workbook.

One final note on perfectionism. Remember, this one is big for so many of us in the helping field. It stems from a lifetime of conditioning to think that perfectionism is something we should strive for. As an adult who has invested nearly a decade into my self-therapeutic work, I can tell you that perfectionism is at the root of most of my cognitive distortions. I think I have always viewed perfectionism as my greatest blessing and curse. Now I view it more as a curse that doesn't outweigh the "good" parts of perfectionism.

> *There is no such thing as perfection – not in life and not in people. [Perfectionism] is a trap.*

Share Your Failures

I can feel the collective tension. Sharing failures is a perfectionist's worst nightmare, but it is crucial! Sharing failures may surprise you. Discussing failures in a group can help paint a more realistic portrait of what other people are struggling with and almost always leads to connection rather than disconnection.

Teachers should be able to admit to families when they've made a mistake. Families should be able to share with teachers parenting mistakes with no fear of judgment or error – this is what would make a good collaborative team.

Sharing failures is an excellent way we can be vulnerable and create opportunities for connection. If you have ever read or heard any of Brené Brown's work on connection, you know that vulnerability is at the source of building authentic connections with one another. Brown has researched happiness for more than two decades. Her previous work identified variables that foster happiness (i.e., vulnerability, connection) and things that hinder happiness (i.e., disconnection, shame).

Brown delivered one of the most-watched TEDx™ talks of all time, entitled "The Power of Vulnerability" (2010). If you haven't seen the 3-minute talk, I highly recommend you do (https://www.ted.com/talks/brene_brown_the_power_of_vulnerability?utm_campaign=tedspread&utm_medium=referral&utm_source=tedcomshare).

… sharing your failures may be one of the most difficult and uncomfortable challenges you'll face; however, I believe it will be one of the most worthwhile fights in your life.

In her newest research, published in *Atlas of the Heart: Mapping Meaningful Connection and the Language of Human Experience* (2021), she writes that "naming an experience (failure or shame) doesn't give the experience more power. It gives us the power of understanding, meaning, and choice."

If you feel like an imposter and you have tendencies toward perfectionism, then the thought of sharing your failures may be excruciating. However, I will go on the record and say it'll be one of the most worthwhile fights in your life. Humans have an innate drive to be connected. When we only share or post our accomplishments, it breeds feelings of inadequacy in others. It can sometimes serve the opposite intention of fostering a connection with others. One perception of the various social media platforms aims to stay connected with others. It is a modern form of adult show-and-tell, yet often, people who use these platforms feel inadequate, alienated, and disconnected from others. If we could foster more *real* platforms that discuss trial and tribulations, missteps and blunders, successes AND failures, paradoxically, you would find that more people would feel a sense of belonging or connecting. Sharing our failures allows us to move past feeling inadequate and start healing and relating to one another. If you can see yourself in someone else's struggles, you are more likely to connect authentically.

I've recently discovered a different type of social media, Marco Polo, which is a video messaging app that allows users to send and receive video messages at their convenience. It creates a video chat experience that combines the best aspects of social media with real-time communication. Unlike traditional video calls that require both parties to be present simultaneously, Marco Polo works more like a walkie-talkie, where users can watch and respond to video messages at their own pace. I've been using Marco Polo with a small group of hand-selected family and friends for just a few months and it already feels much more authentic than any other social media platform (for me). This is not an endorsement, but rather just another story of something that worked for me that may work for some of you. Overall, Marco Polo offers a unique and engaging way to stay connected with friends and family through video messaging, making communication more personal and flexible. For those of you who may be unhappy with traditional social media but don't want to be totally disconnected you may want to give Marco Polo (or something like it) a try.

> *If we could foster more real platforms [social media] that discuss trial and tribulations, missteps and blunders, successes AND failures, paradoxically, you will find that more people would feel a sense of belonging or connecting.*

I'm not saying this will be easy, but it is imperative to overcome shame and start connecting in genuine ways. Maybe start small, just a few trusted friends/

colleagues/family members. Try sharing your shame or sharing perceived failures with them. See how it feels to you. See how it feels when someone else does it. How do you react to someone else's failure confessions? How do they respond to you? See how it goes with even one person. From there, you can build your authentic show-and-tell group and see if life feels better moving forward, not pretending life is only accomplishments and successes.

> *... see if life feels better not pretending it is only a series of accomplishments and success.*

I had my first experience fact-checking my thoughts about what others thought of me when I was five weeks postpartum after giving birth to my first child. At the time, I was the Clinic Director for a national ABA organization in Seattle. Until that time, I had been able to do nearly anything that I wanted with my career and thought I had no limits. (Sounds good? Wrong). I was living away from all my family and friends. My husband regularly traveled to China for work. I decided I wanted to return to work in just five short weeks, even though I had a traumatic labor and delivery.

Man, was I ~~dumb~~, I mean uninformed. Given that I was a perfectionist and incredibly hard on myself, I can see how I was doomed to crash. I was burning the candle at both ends and felt like a failure both at home and work. My brilliant therapist suggested that I ask my direct reports at the time how I was doing – what a novel idea and downright nerve-wracking. I was sure that I knew the answer: I was doing a terrible job and letting everyone down. To my complete and utter shock, both of my direct reports were loving and understanding and did NOT view me as a failure. The response, they felt I was "doing too much and weren't sure how they could help." I couldn't believe my ears. They both had nearly the same feedback. It was clear that my perception of myself was wrong and off. It was a powerful exercise. It takes a bit of good faith and bravery, but it's an excellent gut check. I suggest you all do it at least once. Much of Brené Brown's research is on shame and vulnerability, aka the things that get in the way of connecting and, therefore, happiness. I will include some of her work, but I highly recommend reading further.

> *I've missed more than 9,000 shots in my career. I've lost almost 300 games. Twenty-six times I've been trusted to take the game-winning shot and missed. I've failed over and over and over again in my life. And that is why I succeed.*
> *—Michael Jordan*

Accept It

Understand that just because you are learning about imposter feelings and what to do when they crop up doesn't mean that you'll defeat them once and for all. If you get these feelings once in a while, the best you can do is accept that this is normal. When they do show up, you'll know what to do.

Learning about yourself and your tendencies and beginning to challenge anxious or faulty thinking is a great beginning, but don't fool yourself into thinking that you'll ever solve or fix this problem. It takes a lifetime to form these [bad] habits and will take a lifetime to continue to challenge imposter feelings when they arise. Don't fight the feelings; surrender or accept them as natural. You will get better at identifying and challenging them and realize you must learn to accept them as they crop up. The sooner we do, the better we get at getting back on track faster.

Reflection Questions

1. **Understanding Imposter Syndrome**: Have you ever experienced feelings associated with "imposter syndrome" in your personal or professional life? Can you describe a specific instance where you felt like a "fraud" despite evidence of your competence?
2. **Addressing Cognitive Distortions**: Reflecting on your own thoughts and beliefs, can you identify any cognitive distortions or patterns of negative self-talk? How might these distortions be influencing your perception of yourself and your abilities?

3 **Sharing and Connecting**: How often do you share your feelings of self-doubt or inadequacy with trusted individuals in your life? Do you think being more open about these feelings could change your perspective or help you connect more deeply with others who might be experiencing the same feelings?
4 **Celebrating Successes**: Think about a recent accomplishment, big or small, in your life. How did you react to it? Did you allow yourself to celebrate and internalize that success, or did you dismiss or downplay it? How might actively celebrating your successes impact your feelings of imposter syndrome?

23 Empowering Your Mental and Physical Health

Self-Care

Written by Dr. Ly

This final chapter is written from an instructive and compassionate perspective and from a profound place of personal experience and understanding. The chapter is written for a general audience, particularly those who might feel overwhelmed or have neglected self-care in their lives, such as new parents or professionals prone to burnout. It caters to those who are interested in personal development, wellness, and well-being, providing both historical context and practical tools to support self-care routines. By incorporating personal stories and professional insights, the author aims to reach readers who may need encouragement and guidance in prioritizing self-care for a more balanced and healthy life.

> *Health is a state of complete physical, mental, and social wellbeing and not merely the absence of disease.*
> *—World Health Organization*

Lack of Self-Care Story

I was 32 years old when I had my first child. I delayed having children to complete my education and start my career. I lived in several places around the globe, recently moved back to the United States, and was opening a new region for a national autism services company in Seattle, Washington. I was at the top of my game and happy as can be. I had always wanted to live in Seattle and my husband got a job with a large software company right after I got pregnant. I loved where I was living. I loved my job. I felt like life could not be any better. Sure, we didn't have any friends or family members nearby, but that was no concern. "They were just a phone call or a flight away."

My husband and I were fiercely independent and further, I was used to being on my own. He traveled more than half the time to Asia for work. He had accumulated more than 1 million miles flown by the time our baby was one year old and I thought that was an "accomplishment" – and it made me proud. I felt that we could live anywhere in the world. It was "a feat" that I could live on my own and that my independence was admirable. I was self-sufficient and was proud that I could "do anything or figure anything out all by myself."

Given I did not have any family members nearby, I needed to figure out childcare for my new bundle of joy. I allotted myself six weeks of unpaid leave before heading back to work. Given that my baby arrived one week late, it was five weeks postpartum that I returned to work. My initial time taking care of my newborn only confirmed that I wanted and needed to get back to work – back to "normalcy."

That said, I had a very challenging pregnancy and, like many women, had a "not so glamourous" birth experience. The challenges carried through into postpartum and I was ill-prepared for what was to come.

I was used to moving fast – literally and figuratively. I thought if I just read all the books and took all the labor courses, I would be fine. I had a lifetime of experience overpreparing. I would overprepare and feel very confident. That tendency to overprepare and work hard has served me very well in life. I was "successful" by any measure and was used to "grabbing life by the horns and making things happen." "A mover and shaker." I dreamt big, worked my butt off, and life just kept working out. The hard life lesson that I needed to learn was that – while this may have served me in life before children – all bets are off once you add kids. I can almost hear all the parents sighing, nodding in knowing agreement. You THINK you understand before, but nothing can prepare you for the infinitesimal-ness of carrying, giving birth, and raising children.

Even after I hired an au pair (nanny) at five weeks postpartum, I was a darn fool (in hindsight) for thinking that I could "do it all." I can look back and laugh now, but I felt I was hit by a bus after a complicated pregnancy and delivery (no one can prepare you for such an individual experience). I did not bond with my child immediately. I did not have the euphoria that some mothers experience. I was a "bright light" my entire life – others saw me as perpetually happy, smiling, and loving. I was grossly unprepared for what I experienced during the weeks, months, and even years postpartum.

I could not find sleep. Yes, I know, I expected this. I know that new parents sleep very little, but I would literally go five days without a single second of shuteye. My body would not let me sleep. You hear people giving advice, "sleep when they sleep. Right?!" I tried EVERYTHING. I went to my doctor countless times during the first six weeks. They prescribed me first a long list of naturopathic herbs and supplements. Nothing was working. Then we started down a long line of prescription medications, including Ambien – still nothing. I couldn't find sleep and was not enjoying mothering at all. At one point, my au pair handed my new beautiful, healthy baby to me when I came home from work. I felt nothing. I knew this wasn't good, but I had no experience with any type of depressive symptoms.

I knew this feeling wasn't normal. That I should feel something, but I just didn't. I started to dread being alone with my new baby. I wasn't sure if I could take care of her. I was such a mess and way past the point of being tired. I was on edge, jittery, and nervous all of the time. I started having a slower reaction time but also felt like I could jump out of my skin. I later learned this was the result of post-traumatic stress disorder (PTSD). It never occurred to me that I could have PTSD – that's something soldiers get from war, but after later reading the diagnostic criterion, I had nearly every symptom. I started having regular panic attacks.

Things came to a head when my husband and I had the clever idea of sending me to a hotel overnight to "focus on work." We thought that if I could remove myself from my home environment and my home responsibilities that it would help me to get sleep. At first, it started okay. I finally got ahead of my email inbox and ordered room service. But after I finished work for the day, I paused. What do I do now? Without a house, husband, or baby – what do I do? I kid you not; I did not know what to do. My first thought was to relax. Okay, great, but HOW do I do that? I was so out of the practice of "taking care of myself" that I did not know what I needed to relax anymore. Maybe it will sound nuts to some of you, but this resulted from extreme sleep deprivation and a lifetime of prioritizing everyone except myself.

I turned on the TV but would flip through the channels. I was unfamiliar with television programming, but I was also unaware of how different programming affected me. Violence – no good. Action – no good. Comedy – okay, getting closer, but nothing was relaxing. I just kept wracking my brain to figure out how to relax and bring myself into a state of peace and calm.

At the hotel, by myself, I realized that I had gotten way off track with self-care and in fact, maybe I had never been on a path at all. Having my first baby and how it happened forced me to examine my habits, look at myself in the mirror, and realize that I don't protect my self-care. I was utterly naïve about the care of myself. I couldn't even articulate what I needed to feel healthy, happy, balanced, and at peace.

The long story short is that I continued the slow decline which started well before the baby but finally hit a tipping point and eventually crashed. At my lowest, I was suicidal. This was very scary for both my husband and me and I hope none of you experience it.

After this episode, it was clear that I needed professional help. When I finally got in to see a mental health professional, she recommended a good physician who had experience with mental and women's health, Dr. Mary. She was precisely what I needed. After six weeks with Dr. Mary, I was back on track.

Through many years of therapy and the combination of the "right" meds, I was back to myself again. To those who may go through your version of this scenario, I want to remind you to keep your chin up and try to tune in to what your body (and brain) are telling you. These things are NOT figments of our imagination. The sooner we acknowledge that our biology and physiology run the show, the better. We can't "mind over matter" all things. I delayed getting help because I was too proud or concerned about taking medications. I'm so glad that I listened to Dr. Mary. Ten years later, I've lived in five new cities; however, I will always do telehealth with Dr. Mary. She helped me find steadiness again and I will never forget my state when I arrived in her office. To me, she is an angel.

I now know self-care in terms of the World Health Organization Seven Pillars – health, mental well-being, physical activity, healthy eating, risk avoidance, good hygiene, and responsible use of products/services/medicines. Back then, I was guilty of not doing nearly all of them. Perhaps I was doing okay with risk avoidance, but I was empty on all of the other pillars.

Could all of this have been avoided had I known the value of self-care and prioritized it when I was a new mother? I honestly don't know, but it certainly would have been worth it to try and avoid such a scary breakdown of the self.

I don't think self-care can be understated when I say that self-care serves as THE foundation for how we show up in the world. Once you understand that self-care serves as your foundation, you will realize that whether we prioritize it or not determines how we show up in the world. Do you want a strong, healthy foundation or a shabby crumbling one? What we choose determines how we will best be able to interact with other humans and engage in life's activities. It is NOT a luxury item to be reserved for special occasions but is as essential as the air we breathe.

Self-Care is not a luxury item to be reserved for special occasions but is as essential as the air we breathe.

Stop here – repeat that last sentence as many times as you need until it sinks in.

When you fall off track – getting irritated more easily, quick to anger, frustrated, moody, not your best self – you are likely not attending to your self-care.

I hear you! You THINK that you are "good," you think you are "fine," but then you start down that slippery slope of stress and only after you're well down the slope or crashed at the bottom do you realize, "Oops, I haven't done much self-care lately" (hand raise) – been there.

I want to start a conversation about this and wish all of you to continue these essential conversations throughout your personal and professional lives. Lori and I think that the two covariates we presented in this book – relationships and self-care – are two crucial keys to being successful with the individuals we work with AND improving the lives of all those who care for individuals with special needs.

Once you understand self-care serves as your foundation, you will realize that whether we prioritize it or not determines how we show up in the world.

Who Is Attracted to the Field of Special Needs?

To make a gross overgeneralization, the vast majority of us in our field are bleeding hearts. In other words, we CARE – often, we care A LOT. Not that there is no exception (there always are), but most of our personalities do fall into the "caring" type. Caring types tend to prioritize the needs of others before their own needs. To fall into this caring personality type often leads to burnout and is generally not a good thing for self-care over time.

Exhaustion, meltdown, crash, fatigue, depression, mental collapse, and nervous breakdown are all terms that describe what I am referring to as "burnout." The most encompassing definition of this term and how I am using it in this book is American Psychological Association's (APA) definition which defines "burnout" as follows:

> Physical, emotional, or mental exhaustion accompanied by decreased motivation, lowered performance, and negative attitudes towards oneself and others. It results from performing at a high level until stress and tension, especially from extreme and prolonged physical or mental exertion or an overburdening workload, take their toll. Burnout occurs regularly in professionals who work in service-oriented vocations (e.g., social workers, teachers, etc.) and experience chronic high levels of stress.

Evolution of the Current Self-Care Movement

Self-Care is NOT a new term; it has only recently crossed over into the mainstream in recent years. The Civil Rights and Women's Movements in American history put the concept of "self-care" on the map. The idea here was to attempt to flip the medical model on its head, making it more preventive rather than corrective, and highlight that we can and should "take our healthcare into our own hands."

Around the 1960s, public attitudes began changing or evolving, becoming more "wellness" minded and focused more on improving the quality of one's life. People in the West slowly started hearing phrases like "wellness" and "holistic" and adapting them to their respective lives.

Why Is Self-Care History Important?

Understanding the origins of self-care and where it is now helps us understand why it is becoming increasingly relevant as society changes and demands on people increase. There is a need to update our conceptualization of self-care to reflect the needs of the next generation. It will and should look different depending on the culture you exist within and the individual person. Consider the gender roles of your parents – who did what and who carried what burdens? You likely have different gender roles than your parents held. Are you married or single? Do you have children or not? How you divide and maintain your roles and responsibilities plays a considerable role in how or whether these roles cause you stress.

> *There is a need to update our conceptualization of self-care to reflect the needs of the next generation. It will and should look different depending on the culture you exist within and the individual person.*

Figure 23.1 Seven Pillars of Self-Care
Source: International Self-Care Foundation. (September 10, 2016).

The World Health Organization (WHO) has produced three definitions of "self-care" since its inception. The WHO 1998 definition is:

> Self-Care is what people do for themselves to establish and maintain health and prevent and deal with illness. It is a broad concept encompassing hygiene (general and personal), nutrition (type and quality of food eaten), lifestyle (sporting activities, leisure, etc.), environmental factors (living conditions, social habits, etc.), socio-economic factors (income level, cultural beliefs, etc.) and self-medication.

Based on the WHO's 1998 definition of Self-Care, the International Self-Care Foundation created the "Seven Pillars of Self-Care," see Figure 23.1 (reprinted with permission).

Seven Pillars of Self-Care

The following is a summary of the seven distinct pillars as described by the International Self-Care Foundation:

1 **Health Literacy** – the capacity of individuals to obtain, process, and understand basic health information and services needed to make appropriate health decisions.
2 **Mental Well-being** – includes life satisfaction, optimism, self-esteem, mastery, feeling in control, having a purpose in life, and a sense of belonging and support.

3 **Physical Activity** – need for, and benefit gained from, regular physical activity.
4 **Healthy Eating** – having a nutritious, balanced diet with appropriate caloric intake.
5 **Risk Avoidance/Mitigation** avoidance or reduction of behaviors that directly increase the risk of disease or death.
6 **Good Hygiene** – actions and behaviors that contribute to good hygiene and the prevention of infectious diseases and illnesses.
7 **Rational/Responsible Use of Products, Services, Diagnostics, and Medicines** – knowledgeable, safe, and effective use of health products and services by individuals to better manage health.

As times change and we enter uncharted cultural/historical territory, it is vital to recognize how we must adapt and adjust our definition of how to care for ourselves to meet our personal needs. I present the WHO definition and the International Self-Care Foundation Seven Pillar model to demonstrate how we can help support our self-care.

Self-care is *not* getting a massage once a month or every six months. Self-care is *not* taking a shower (I'm talking to YOU, new parents). Self-care is *not* taking ONE mental health day after being burnt out. Self-care is *not* going to the gym when you're tense.

Self-care IS technically all of those things mentioned here; however, the distinction is that you must do your self-care regularly to serve a rejuvenation function. In other words, we must learn how to:

(1) learn the ways we can take care of ourselves (consider the Seven Pillars)
(2) find a way to incorporate them into our daily habits
(3) protect our self-care as essential and critical

I like to think of self-care as an empty tank or a vessel, where YOU are the empty vessel. Imagine that everything you do or do *not* do either has a positive impact on your system, whereby it is rejuvenating/recharging, or it has a negative effect, whereby it takes/depletes energy from your system. You will know when you are full because you feel good, happy, satisfied, energetic, and ready to take on the world. When you are empty or getting nearer to empty, you will know when you feel nervous, jittery, anxious, depressed, irritable, frustrated, and so on. The key is to tune in early in the process when you start feeling "a little nervous" or "a little irritable" – the odds are that you have been taking care of the needs of others and not taking care of your own needs. Tune into your own needs and you will be able to serve others better. I know this will resonate with anyone who struggles with self-care.

If you can learn to take care of yourself better, you will be able to take care of others better. That's self-care as it pertains to collaborative support teams.

If we can learn to show up, know, honor, and protect our human right to take care of the self, we will show up stronger and healthier for those we serve and love.

If we can learn to show up, know, honor, and protect our human right to take care of the self, we will show up stronger and healthier for those we serve and love.

Imagine this, not just for our students but for all the people belonging to the collaborative team. After losing myself after having a child, I started getting serious about my self-care. For some reason (and I know many of you will relate), life became more clear once I became a parent. If I don't take care of myself, it directly affects those around me; however, if I DO take care of myself, that also impacts those around me, but with a positive impact. You choose where you would rather be.

Not to say that recognizing the need for self-care translates into instant action. Sadly, we will probably need to tune into it at some level for our entire lives, but it does become more and more natural to advocate for the things that have a rejuvenating effect and learn to let go of the things that have a depleting effect. The things that serve us versus the things that do not serve us.

If you want or need additional help and want to dig deeper, allow me to introduce someone I have found to be very inspiring and insightful on my journey. Dr. Nicole LePera, widely known as the "Holistic Psychologist," is a clinical psychologist who champions the connection between mind and body in mental health treatment. She founded the online community "The Holistic Psychologist," where she promotes self-healing practices that include mindfulness, meditation, nutrition, and environmental awareness. This approach broadens the scope beyond traditional therapy techniques.

She is a prominent figure on social media platforms, especially Instagram. Dr. LePera has attracted millions of followers who engage with her regular posts, videos, and live sessions. Her content often includes practical tips, inspirational quotes, and personal anecdotes, making mental health and self-care more accessible and relatable to a broad audience.

If you are interested, she wrote a powerful book entitled *How to Do the Work: Recognizing Your Patterns, Heal From Your Past, and Create Your Self*

(2021) as well as online courses (https://theholisticpsychologist.com) and speaking engagements (see YouTube), she empowers individuals worldwide to take control of their mental and emotional well-being. Her teachings, rooted in conscious and intentional living, draw from her personal journey to holistic health.

A word of caution – while her integrative approach has resonated with many and inspired a movement toward holistic mental health, some professionals are concerned about her encouragement of self-healing without expert supervision, which may not be suitable for everyone, particularly those with more severe mental health conditions. If you are further along in your therapeutic journey, you may find her work helpful; however, if you are new to therapy or self-healing care, please take note if anything is particularly triggering and definitely solicit the help of a professional.

I mention Dr. LePera's because of the innovative work she's doing and her prominent social media presence, which has expanded the conversation around mental health and self-care and placed her at the forefront of a growing movement that emphasizes a more comprehensive and individualized approach to well-being.

Listen, if you are at this point and wondering what the big deal is, congratulations, you are probably part of the rare few that have a handle on your self-care. If you self-regulate, you feel happy, healthy, balanced, steady, and so on, on the regular – just keep doing what you're doing, and bravo! Good on you, and congratulations on winning the self-care lottery. If you are among the vast majority of us (yes, me included) that struggle (sometimes profoundly) with self-care – just keep showing up. Try the tools/strategies listed in this chapter until something sticks, or you can create enough healthy habits to feel most centered, grounded, and steady in your daily lives.

Where Do We Go From Here?

I am taking stock of all the activities and relationships in my life. First, I will create an awareness of these relationships and activities and ask myself, do the individuals I engage with and activities I participate in give or take energy from me? Determining what people and activities serve me will help clarify my choices – who I spend my time with and what activities I choose to do each day.

You are the one responsible for describing, articulating, maintaining, and protecting your self-care, your priorities, your peace.

This doesn't mean that you ONLY do the positive activities or hang with the positive people, but it helps to be more conscious of how we spend our time. So, if you decide to be with someone who generally depletes you or an activity that you find draining, be mindful that you will need to make up for this loss of energy. I find it helpful to think of this exercise as "keeping yourself on track." Find where your center is – what activities and people bring you joy, peace, calm, inspiration, and try to stay there. Inevitably, life and choices will throw you, but try recentering yourself once you realize this.

The most powerful part of this exercise is that you are responsible for DESCRIBING, ARTICULATING, MAINTAINING, AND PROTECTING your self-care, priorities, and peace.

Do you understand why this is so important? The way we show up to the world influences EVERYTHING.

[mind blown]

Imagine feeling like you have a handle on your peace. Sounds idealistic and impossible? It is not impossible; it is possible – one step at a time. If you're struggling, it may be one day, one minute, one second, or one breath at a time, but it IS POSSIBLE. Start where you are and just keep showing up for yourself.

For me, it's helpful to do mindfulness or meditation practice. Suppose you don't currently have one or are unsure where to start – start where you are. Just set aside time (can be as simple as 1–2 minutes) where you tune inward and acknowledge how you are feeling and try concentrating on your breath. Often this is enough to bring you a sense of awareness and calm; however, if you are naturally more nervous/anxious or have a more racing mind, perhaps try guided meditation (that's what I do). Focusing on your breathing will help keep you centered and stay on track. Also, guided meditation typically has a focus or intention, so if you're struggling with chronic pain or a racing mind, you can focus on that. Additionally, most mindfulness practices utilize all our senses to ground us. For example, answering the following questions – what do you hear? Taste? Smell? See? Touch? There are many good mindfulness meditation programs out there. The ones I have personally used and recommend often are Head Space, Curable, Calm, Sleepiest, and Tapping Solutions. All are readily available in most app stores.

Hal Elrod describes other beneficial tools for setting your self-care routine up for success in his book *The Miracle Morning*. You are welcome to read the entire book, but here is a summary to get you started. In his book, Elrod laid out a six-step morning routine utilizing "Life SAVERS." SAVERS stands for Silence, Affirmations, Visualizations, Exercise, Reading, and Scribing. He suggests doing the following each morning immediately after you wake up:

- **Silence** – Start every morning with a period of purposeful silence.
- **Affirmations** – Program yourself to be confident and successful in everything you do.
- **Visualizations** – Imagine what you want to achieve and mentally rehearse what you need to achieve it.
- **Exercise**

- **Reading** – Learn from the experts and model successful people who have already achieved what you want.
- **Scribing** – Writing enables you to document your insights and any areas of opportunity.

For this book and how I utilize Elrod's "miracle morning" is the "6-Minute Miracle" (for busy people). In "miracle morning," the author goes into great detail about each of these areas, covers the how-to of each, and uncovers obstacles that many people have. Please read it if you are interested in more about establishing your miracle morning. Here's how my adaptation of the "6-Minute Miracle" looks:

1 Sit quietly in purposeful silence/meditation (1 minute)
2 Read your affirmations (or mantras) aloud (1 minute)
3 Visualize what it will look and feel like when you reach your goals (1 minute)
4 Write down (or say aloud) things that you're grateful for or proud of (1 minute)
5 Read a self-help (or inspirational) book (1 minute or 1 page)
6 Move your body – stretching (1 minute)

Six minutes, people. You can accomplish great things and set the tone for your day in six minutes. Try it for two weeks, every single day. See for yourself how it feels. I used to do it every morning. Now, I only do some tenants. For example, I no longer read for a minute in the morning because I read extensively at night. When I was doing all six tenants, that was the only time I did those things. I also no longer meditate in the morning because I do a more extended meditation later in the day. I do try to sit in silence, though. Try it, make a new habit, learn the six tenants, then decide what works for you – just another tool in your self-care toolbelt.

For exercise, if you already have your preferred way of getting exercise, keep doing that. If you don't currently exercise and are overwhelmed at the thought of trying to start an exercise routine, I have a suggestion. I played sports my entire adult life and was able to get my exercise that way, and then my knees started failing me … six surgeries later, I am no longer able to do the things I once did. This is where yoga comes in.

Yoga probably elicits a wide range of concepts for people. Let me tell you what yoga is for me. Plain and simple, it is stretching. There are many different types of yoga – Yin, Hatha, Vinyasa, and so on. Most people aren't aware that these different types are even available to you, and usually, you can find a style that suits you better than others.

Additionally, using props (bolster, bricks, strap, etc.) can dramatically improve your experience. One of my favorite yoga teachers explains that props "help you change your relationship with the floor." I used to think that props were for more advanced forms of yoga (probably because I didn't know how to use them), but later learned that they help you MODIFY poses to meet you

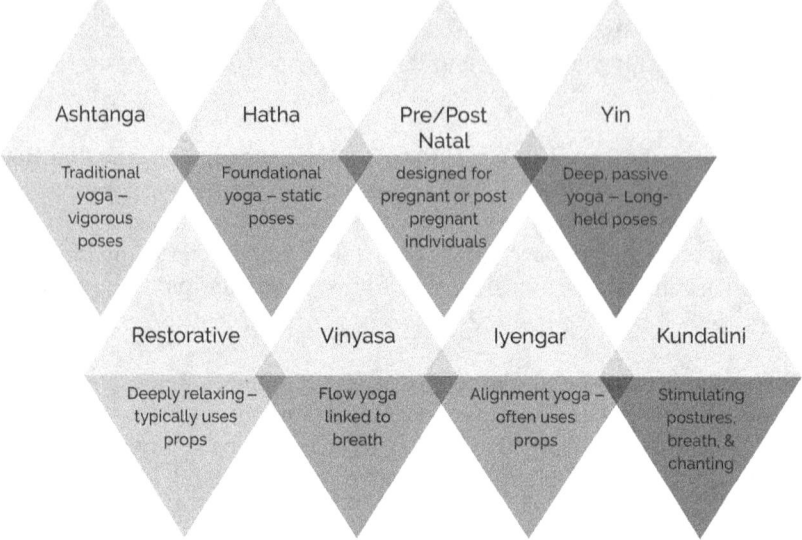

Figure 23.2 Different Styles of Yoga

where you are. After multiple surgeries and with limited mobility, yoga was one of the most valuable tools in keeping me active but not causing unnecessary stress or pain. If you don't currently have an exercise routine, or your current exercise routine isn't working for you, I encourage you to try different styles of yoga (Figure 23.2).

I prefer to have a home yoga practice, but others may want to go to a studio or gym. As with the other areas of self-care, ask yourself what suits you better and do that. I use an on-demand yoga platform that I've been using for many years, called YogaGlo (www.yogaglo.com). I used it through pre/post-natal, post-surgery recovery, and now ongoing as I age. My preferred types of yoga are yin and restorative. It's more for stress/tension reduction and helps circulation, but there are types to meet all needs.

Exercise for physical health is something different. Aside from yoga, activities like walking, running, biking, swimming, or sports are all great ways to get some activity in. Exercise, as I refer to it in self-care, means movement. When I discuss exercise in this way, I refer to finding a way that works for you to move your body. Additionally, when you decide which form of movement you prefer, it doesn't take much to have a meaningful effect on your mental wellbeing. As little as five minutes done daily will have a significant impact. Try it and commit to it for at least two weeks, five minutes a day and see for yourself. There are no excuses. Once you are serious enough about your self-care and prioritize it, you will figure it out. Remember, we outlined how to make movement possible even for the busiest of people; and those who don't like traditional exercise in the gym. Can you invest five minutes into your daily wellness tank?

In sum, self-care is an ongoing, ever-evolving journey that requires conscious intention, persistent practice, and gentle forgiveness. It's about recognizing and honoring our needs, ensuring that we are not only serving others but also replenishing our energy. The journey might be challenging and seemingly daunting, but every step forward counts. Whether you're meditating, practicing yoga, reading a book, or just taking time to breathe deeply and relax, each action contributes to your self-care journey. The tools and strategies detailed in this chapter offer a starting point, but ultimately, it's about finding what works best for you. Remember, your self-care directly impacts not only your own well-being, but it also affects those around you. The power to create a positive ripple effect lies in your hands. So keep showing up, keep trying, keep nurturing yourself. With every step, with every breath, you're making a difference. Just remember, the most significant investment you can ever make is in yourself.

Reflection Questions

1. **Connection to Self-Care Pillars**: After reading the Seven Pillars of Self-Care, which pillar resonates with you the most right now and why? Conversely, which pillar do you feel you might be neglecting or could further improve upon in your life?
2. **Self-Care vs. Self-Care Activities**: The chapter highlights the distinction between sporadic self-care activities and the continuous practice of self-care. Reflect on your current self-care habits. Are there activities you consider as self-care but only practice occasionally? How might you adjust these to serve a more consistent and rejuvenating role in your life?
3. **Energy Givers and Takers**: Reflect on the activities and relationships in your life. Which ones predominantly give you energy and which ones predominantly take energy away from you? Are there any shifts or changes you might consider to achieve a more harmonious balance?
4. **Mindfulness and Meditation**: The author emphasizes the importance of mindfulness and meditation in their self-care routine. Have you tried either of these practices before? If yes, what was your experience? If no, which of the suggested methods or tools might you consider trying and why?

We have reached the end of the book. You have learned about Discovering and Navigating the world of having or working with someone with special learning needs. We now have started the work of seeing the world from shared perspectives and, in doing that, have much more compassion and understanding for the multiple "players" on our Collective Efficacy team. In doing this, we realize the importance of establishing and maintaining authentic relationships as being essential for working collaboratively on support teams. We recognized that improving the relationships we have with one another dramatically affects our ability to be as helpful as possible in our efforts with our students; further, if we choose to overlook this third variable, it's likely to serve as a barrier to success.

The other barrier that is often overlooked but arguably matters the most is self-care. The importance of self-care cannot be overstated, as this is the foundation for how we show up in the world. We learned how the World Health Organization defines self-care and how the American Psychological Association defines burnout and we see the connection between caring for the self and burnout. We learned that how we take care of ourselves has an immediate and direct impact on our mental health and how we interact with all those around us. We gave you many different tools and resources to embark upon your own self-care journey.

We outlined several "Pillars of Self-Care" described by the International Self-Care Foundation and understand that we must consider all of them at some level to address the whole gamut of our self-care needs. We attempted to simplify and condense many concepts and themes to make them as useable and achievable as possible.

We hope you have found the book to be helpful. We also hope you continue to share what you've learned with your family, friends, and colleagues to help keep these conversations going and evolving. Thank you for taking the time and we wish you all the best in your conquest to implement these strategies in your daily lives.

References

American Psychiatric Association. (2013). *Diagnostic and statistical manual of mental disorders* (5th ed.). American Psychiatric Publishing.

American Psychiatric Association. (2022). *Diagnostic and statistical manual of mental disorders* (5th ed., text rev.). Retrieved from https://www.psychiatry.org/

Assistive Ware B.V. (2023). Proloquo 2 Go AAC (v. 8.0) [Mobile Application Software]. Retrieved from Apple App Store.

Bandura, A. (1997). *Self-efficacy: The exercise of control*. W.H. Freeman and Company.

Begeny, J.C., & Martens, B.K. (2007). Inclusionary education in Italy: A literature review and call for more empirical research. *Remedial and Special Education, 28*, 80–94.

Boll, L. (2018, February 15). He's Got a Golden Ticket. LoriBoll.me. https://www.loriboll.me/hes-got-a-golden-ticket/

Bondy, A., & Frost, L. (2001). The picture exchange communication system. *Behavior Modification, 25*(5), 725–744. https://doi.org/10.1177/0145445501255004

Bourne, E. J. (2015). *The Anxiety & Phobia workbook – Sixth edition*. New Harbinger Publications.

Brown, B. (2010a, June). The power of vulnerability. *TEDxHouston*. Retrieved from https://www.ted.com/talks/brene_brown_the_power_of_vulnerability

Brown, B. (2010b). *The gifts of imperfection: Let go of who you think you're supposed to be and embrace who you are*.

Brown, B. (2021). *Atlas of the heart: Mapping meaningful connection and the language of human experience* (1st ed.). Random House.

Brown v. Board of Education, 347 U.S. 483 (1954).

Brucker, P.O. (1994). The advantages of inclusion for students with learning disabilities. *Journal of Learning Disabilities, 27*, 581–582.

Burns, M. K., Jimerson, S. R., VanDerHeyden, A. M., & Deno, S. L. (2016). Toward a unified response-to-intervention model: Multi-tiered systems of support. In S. R. Jimerson, M. K. Burns, & A. M. VanDerHeyden (Eds.), *Handbook of response to intervention: the science and practice of multitiered systems of support* (2nd ed., pp. 719–732). New York, NY: Springer.

Calm.com, Inc. (2023). Calm: Meditation and Sleep Stories [Mobile app]. App Store. https://www.calm.com/

Center for MTSS. (2023). https://mtss4success.org/

Center for RTI. (2023). https://rti4success.org/

Center on Response to Intervention & National Center on Intensive Intervention. (2014). *Response to intervention glossary of terms*. Washington, DC. Retrieved January 23, 2019, from https://rti4success.org/sites/default/files/CenterOnRTIGlossary.pdf

Centers for Disease Control and Prevention. (2020). Data and statistics on children's mental health. https://www.cdc.gov/childrensmentalhealth/data.html

Clubfoot (talipes Equinovarus). Symptoms, Diagnosis and Treatment. (2021). Retrieved from https://www.nationwidechildrens.org/conditions/clubfoot-talipes-equinovarus

Curable Inc. (2023). Curable: Chronic Pain Relief [Mobile app]. App Store. https://www.curablehealth.com/

Donohoo, J., Hattie, J., & Eells, R. (2018). The power of collective efficacy. *Educational Leadership*, 75(6), 41. ASCD.

Eells, R. (2011). Meta-analysis of the relationship between collective efficacy and student achievement (Unpublished doctoral dissertation). Loyola University of Chicago.

Elrod, H. (2014). *The miracle morning: The not-so-obvious secret guaranteed to transform your life before 8am*. Hal Elrod International.

Flannery, K. A., & Wisner-Carlson, R. (2020). Autism and Education. *Child and Adolescent Psychiatric Clinics of North America*, 29(2), 319–343. https://doi.org/10.1016/j.chc.2019.12.005

Greater Good Science Center. (2011). John Gottman: How to build trust - YouTube. Retrieved March 27, 2022, from https://www.youtube.com/watch?v=rgWnadSi91s

Greene, R. W. (2008). *Lost at school: Why our kids with behavioral challenges are falling through the cracks and how we can help them (First Scribner hardcover)*. Scribner.

Greene, R. W. (2010a). *The explosive child: A new approach for understanding and parenting easily frustrated, chronically inflexible children* (Rev. and updated ed.). New York, NY: HarperPaperbacks.

Greene, R. W. (2010b). Collaborative problem solving. In R. C. Murrihy, A. D. Kidman, & T. H. Ollendick (Eds.), *Clinical handbook of assessing and treating conduct problems in youth* (pp. 193–220). Springer Science + Business Media. https://doi.org/10.1007/978-1-4419-6297-3_8

Hampton, D. (2016, March). The Quickest Way to Change How You Feel is to Change How You Think. *The Best Brain Possible*. Retrieved from https://thebestbrainpossible.com/

Hartney, E. (2021, November). 10 Cognitive Distortions Identified in CBT. *Verywell Mind*. Retrieved from https://www.verywellmind.com

Hattie, J. [John Hattie]. (2018, August 27). LEAP Principal Conference 2018 [Video]. YouTube. https://www.youtube.com/watch?v=UCMV692itfg

Hattie, J. A. C., & Zierer, K. (2018). *Ten mindframes for visible learning: Teaching for success*. Routledge.

Headspace Inc. (2023). Headspace: Meditation & Sleep [Mobile app]. App Store. https://www.headspace.com/

Individuals with Disabilities Education Act (IDEA). (n.d.). OAR 581-015-2080.

Individuals with Disabilities Education Act (IDEA), 20 U.S.C. § 1400 (2004).

International Self-Care Foundation. (September 10, 2016). The Seven Pillars of Self-Care. Retrieved from https://isfglobal.org/practise-self-care/the-seven-pillars-of-self-care/

Kennedy Krieger Institute. (2017, May 17). Sleep Problems Linked to More Severe Autism Symptoms. Kennedy Krieger Institute. https://www.kennedykrieger.org/stories/interactive-autism-network-ian/sleep-problems-linked-more-severe-autism-symptoms

Kübler-Ross, E. (1969). *On death and dying*. Macmillan Company.
Ladau, E. (2015, August). What I want future teachers to know about disability. Retrieved from https://emilyladau.com/2015/08/what-i-want-future-teachers-to-know-about-disability/
Ladau, E. (2021). *Demystifying disability: What to know, what to say, and how to be an ally* [Paperback - Illustrated]. Penguin Random House.
LePera, N. (2021). *How to do the work: Recognize your patterns, heal from your past, and create your self*. Harper Wave.
Lord, C., Rutter, M., DiLavore, P. C., & Risi, S. (2012). *Autism diagnostic observation schedule – Second edition (ADOS-2)*. Western Psychological Services.
Maddox, B. B. (2021). Accuracy of the ADOS-2 in identifying autism among adults with complex psychiatric conditions. In *Encyclopedia of autism spectrum disorders* (pp. 42–43). https://doi.org/10.1007/978-3-319-91280-6_102372
Mader, J. (2017, March 3). Teacher training is failing students with disabilities. *The Atlantic*. https://www.theatlantic.com/education/archive/2017/03/how-teacher-training-hinders-special-needs-students/518286/
McBean, A.L. & Schlosnagle, L. (2016). Sleep, health and memory: comparing parents of typically developing children and parents of children with special health-care needs. *Journal of Sleep Research, 25*, 78–87. https://doi.org/10.1111/jsr.12329
McElhanon, B. O., McCracken, C., Karpen, S., & Sharp, W. G. (2014). Gastrointestinal symptoms in autism spectrum disorder: A meta-analysis. *Pediatrics, 133*(5), 872–883. https://doi.org/10.1542/peds.2013-3995
McLeskey, J., & Waldron, N. L. (2007). Making differences ordinary in inclusive classrooms. *Intervention in School and Clinic, 42*, 162–168.
National Association of State Boards of Education (NASBE). (1992). National Longitudinal Study. The Bureau of Labor Statistics (BLS) of the U.S. Department of Labor.
Novak, E. (2021). What is UDL? [Infographic]. *Novak Education*. Retrieved from https://www.novakeducation.com/blog/what-is-udl-infographic
Orbe-Austin, L., & Orbe-Austin, R. (2020). *Own your own greatness: overcome imposter syndrome, beat self-doubt, and succeed in life*. Ulysses Press.
Palmer, C. (2021, June). How to overcome impostor phenomenon. *Monitor on Psychology, 52*(4). Retrieved from http://www.apa.org/monitor/2021/06/cover-impostor-phenomenon
Perera, N. (2021, January 13). British vs American Education Systems: Reference to IGCSE and SAT. *Tutopiya*. Retrieved October 2, 2021, from https://www.tutopiya.com/blog/british-vs-american-education-systems-with-reference-to-igcse-and-sat/
Robins, D. L., Casagrande, K., Barton, M., Chen, C. M., Dumont-Mathieu, T., & Fein, D. (2014). Validation of the modified checklist for Autism in toddlers, revised with follow-up (M-CHAT-R/F). *Pediatrics, 133*(1), 37–45. https://doi.org/10.1542/peds.2013-1813
Robins, D. L., Fein, D., & Barton, M. (2009). *The modified checklist for autism in toddlers, Revised with follow-up (M-CHAT-R/F)*. Self-published.
Rogers, J. (1993). The inclusion revolution. *Research Bulletin, Phi Delta Kappa, 11*, 1–6.
Sicherman, N., Loewenstein, G., Tavassoli, T., & Buxbaum, J. D. (2017). Grandma knows best: Family structure and age of diagnosis of autism spectrum disorder. *Autism, 22*(3), 368–376. https://doi.org/10.1177/1362361316679632
Sleepiest, Inc. (2023). Sleepiest: Sleep Well & Relax [Mobile app]. App Store. https://www.sleepiest.com/

Tapping Solution, LLC. (n.d.). Tapping Solutions: EFT Tapping [Mobile app]. App Store. https://www.thetappingsolution.com/

The Holistic Psychologist. Retrieved August 21, 2023, from https://theholisticpsychologist.com/

U.S. Department of Education, Office for Civil Rights. (2016). 2013–2014 civil rights data collection: A first look.

U.S. Department of Education, Office of Special Education and Rehabilitative Services. (2017). 39th annual report to Congress on the implementation of the Individuals with Disabilities Education Act, 2017. Washington, D.C.

Voress, J. K., & Maddox, T. (2012). *Developmental assessment of young children* (2nd ed.). PRO-ED Inc.

YogaGlo. (2023). Home. Retrieved June 24, 2023, from https://www.yogaglo.com

Zones of Regulation. (2023). https://zonesofregulation.com/

Zumeta Edmonds, R. (2016). Ask the expert: Multi-tiered system of supports – MTSS vs RtI [Video]. https://rti4success.org/video/mtss-and-rti-are-often-usedinterchangeably-what-it-separates-them

Index

Pages in *italics* refer to figures and pages in **bold** refer to tables.

advocacy: in diagnosis process 27; having a special needs child 18, 29, 59, 90; for inclusion 65; in school transitions 81; for student needs 29, 33

Applied Behavior Analysis (ABA): application and perspectives 112–113

assessment: best practice guidelines *37*; clinical process 34–35, *36–37*; complications 28–29; considerations 20–25; Dr. Ly's process 34–39; role of informants *37*; school process 43–44; *see also* MTSS

ATTUNE 139, *140*, 142

attention-deficit/hyperactivity disorder (ADHD), prevalence **31**

autism spectrum disorder (ASD): ABA with ASD 112; assessment 17, 21–22; early signs 18; in general education 50–52; parent perspective and emotional impact 59–60, 63–66; prevalence **31**; screening 31–32; *see also* grief; societal reactions, dealing with 63–65

Bandura A. *see* Collective Efficacy

burnout 164; propensity for caring professionals 164; *see also* self-care

"casting a wide net" *see* screening

Child Find 16, 88

child psychopathologies overview 30

cognitive abilities: assessment of 34–35, 39–40, *41–43*; relative to mean ability, on standard normal curve *41–43*

collaboration: collaborative relationships 12–14, 139, 168; between parents, educators, therapists 9–14, 131–133

Collaborative and Proactive Solutions 118

Collective Efficacy: Albert Bandura Research 9–10; building and creating 30, 33, 53, 58, 143; concept of and background 9–11; educational application 11–14; research; *see also* Eells, R.; Hattie, J.; student achievement influence on 11

communication: miscommunications 125, 140; between parents and educators 71–74, 97, *98*, 127–129, 134; *see also* parent-educator communication; special education; strategies 127–129; technology, impact on 127, 134; tools, utilization of 134; value of 4

conflict: difficult conversations, strategies for 143–146; management 139; resolution 139, 143, 145

diagnosis: complications 27–29; confirmed, contradicted, inconclusive *38–39*; considerations 20–25; grief 63–65; labeling, pros and cons 21; obtaining *38–39*; from parent perspective 15–19, 59–65; pediatricians, role in diagnosis 21–22; public vs. private evaluations 22–25; qualities of good diagnostician 28

difficult conversations *see* conflict, difficult conversations

Index

disability: "golden ticket" notion 106; misconceptions about 106–108; societal perceptions 107; teacher and parent perspectives, comparison 105–108
diagnostic process *see* assessment
Donohoo., J. 9–11, 136

educational setting: bias in, addressing 116–119; goodness of fit 75–76; school placement **85**; special education system, evaluation 77–78; *see also* special education
education terminology *see* special education, acronym
empathy 13, 58, 66, 118–119, 129, 140
Eells, R. 10

Gatekeepers in diagnosis 27; diagnostician; *see also* diagnosis, qualities of good diagnostician; parent and diagnostician expectations 28–29
general education: inclusive education, training for 52–58; special needs students, integration resources 54, 55, 57; supporting general education teachers; *see also* inclusion; teacher perspectives on inclusion 50–52
"golden ticket" 105–106; *see also* disability, misconceptions about
Gottman Institute The 139–140
Greene, R. 116–118, 132
grief 63–65

Holistic Psychologist The 168–169
Hattie, J. 11–13

Individual Education Plan (IEP) 53, *54*; educational terminology *see* special education acronyms and impacts on parents
imposter syndrome: how to overcome 148–158; what it is 147–148
inclusion: benefits of 77; call to xiv–xv; difference between mainstreaming 76–77; inclusive learning environment *see* UDL; supporting general education teachers 51–53, 58
intellectual disability (ID), prevalence **31**

Kubler Ross, E. 62

LePera, N. *see* Holistic Psychologist

MCHAT-R/F™ 31–32
mental health, physical health connection, *166*, 167–169, *172*; *see also* self-care
Multi-Tier System of Support (MTSS): background 32; framework 46, *47*; key tenets of intervention 79; resources for implementation 48; Tier 1 47; Tier 2 47; Tier 3 48

Novak, K. xiv, 56–57

Picture Exchange Communications System (PECS) 89–90
prevalence rates: autism spectrum disorder (ASD) **31**; attention-deficit/hyperactivity disorder (ADHD) **31**; intellectual disability (ID) **31**; specific learning disability (SLD) **31**
psychological effects, discussion; *see also* self-care
professional relationships: consultants, relationship dynamics 100–101; professional collaboration, importance 101–103

relationships: building positive relationships 120–124; empathy, role in education 129; student engagement, improving 123; student-teacher interactions 123, 129

school transitions 81–87; international schools, challenges in 81–84, **85–86**; special learning accommodation 55, 83, 85; student rejection of admission, reasons for **85–86**
school setting, diagnostic process *see* MTSS
screening: "casting a wide net" 35, *36*, 44; tools, various types 31–33
self-care: application to collaborative teams 167–168, 170–173; evolution of modern movement 165; and the Holistic Psychologist 169; importance of 163, 165; imposter syndrome, overcoming; *see also* imposter syndrome; personal growth strategies 168–172, *166*, *172*; psychological effects, discussion 160–164; self-doubt 148, 151; *see also* imposter syndrome; Seven Pillars of Self-Care *166*; WHO definition 166–167

special education: acronyms and impact on parents 71–74; early identification 46–47, 78, 80; evaluation of special education system 77–78; family experience living abroad 16; parent perspective 15; parent-educator communication 72–73

specific learning disability (SLD), prevalence **31**

trust building strategies 94–95, 101, 139–140

teaching approaches: evolution of teaching practices 110–111; professional development, importance of 111; school of thought, old school vs. new school 109–115

Universal Design for Learning (UDL) 56, 57

For Product Safety Concerns and Information please contact our EU representative GPSR@taylorandfrancis.com
Taylor & Francis Verlag GmbH, Kaufingerstraße 24, 80331 München, Germany